Warwickshire County Council

This item is to be returned or renewed before the latest date above. It may be borrowed for a further period if not in demand. **To renew your books:**

- **Phone the 24/7 Renewal Line 01926 499273 or**
- **Visit www.warwickshire.gov.uk/libraries**

Discover ● Imagine● Learn ● *with libraries*

Warwickshire
County Council

Working for
Warwickshire

TEDBooks

Thanks
A
Thousand

A Gratitude Journey
from Bean to Cup

A.J. JACOBS

ILLUSTRATIONS BY CLAIRE MERCHLINSKY

TED Books
Simon & Schuster

London   New York   Toronto   Sydney   New Delhi

TEDBooks

First published in Great Britain by Simon & Schuster UK Ltd, 2018
A CBS COMPANY

First TED Books hardback edition November 2018
TED, the TED logo and TED Books are trademarks of TED Conference, LLC.
TED BOOKS and colophon are registered trademarks of TED Conferences, LLC.
For more information on licensing the TED talk that accompanies this book,
or other content partnerships with TED, please contact TEDBooks@TED.com.

10 9 8 7 6 5 4 3 2 1

Simon & Schuster UK Ltd
1st Floor, 222 Gray's Inn Road
London WC1X 8HB

www.simonandschuster.co.uk
www.simonandschuster.com.au
www.simonandschuster.co.in

Simon & Schuster Australia, Sydney
Simon & Schuster India, New Delhi

A CIP catalogue record for this book
is available from the British Library

Hardback ISBN: 978-1-4711-5605-2
eBook ISBN: 978-1-4711-5606-9

Illustrations by Claire Merchlinsky
Interior design by MGMT.design
Printed and bound by CPI Group (UK) Ltd, Croydon, CR0 4YY

MIX
Paper from
responsible sources
FSC
www.fsc.org   FSC® C020471

Simon & Schuster UK Ltd are committed to sourcing paper
that is made from wood grown in sustainable forests and support the Forest
Stewardship Council, the leading international forest certification organisation.
Our books displaying the FSC logo are printed on FSC certified paper.

To my family.
And everyone else.

CONTENTS

Thanks
A
Thousand

It's a Tuesday morning, and I'm in the presence of one of the most mind-boggling accomplishments in human history. This thing is so astounding in its complexity and scope, it makes the Panama Canal look like a third grader's craft project.

This marvel I see before me is the result of thousands of human beings collaborating across dozens of countries.

It took the combined labor of artists, chemists, politicians, mechanics, biologists, miners, packagers, smugglers, and goatherds.

It required airplanes, boats, trucks, motorcycles, vans, pallets, and shoulders.

It needed hundreds of materials—steel, wood, nitrogen, rubber, silicon, ultraviolet light, explosives, and bat guano.

It has caused great joy but also great poverty and oppression.

It relied upon ancient wisdom and space-age technology, freezing temperatures and scorching heat, high mountains and deep water.

It is my morning cup of coffee.

And I'm grateful for it. Really, really grateful.

It wasn't always so. I tend to take things for granted. For most of my life, I rarely thought about my coffee unless it spilled on my jacket or scalded the roof of my mouth. But the last few months have forced me to change that. Earlier this year, in an attempt to battle my default mental state (generalized annoyance and impatience), I undertook a deceptively simple quest. I pledged to thank every single person who made my cup of coffee possible. I resolved to thank the barista, the farmer who grew the beans, and all those in between.

That turned out to be a hell of a lot of thank-yous. My gratitude quest has taken me across time zones, and up and down the social ladder. It's made me rethink everything from globalism to beavers, from hugs to fonts, from light bulbs to ancient Rome. It's affected my politics, my worldview, and my palate. It's made me feel delight, wonder, guilt, depression, and, of course, a whole bunch of caffeine jitters.

●   ●   ●

How did this quest get started? Well, I've been an admirer of gratitude for several years. It's not an emotion that comes naturally to me. My innate disposition is moderately grumpy, more Larry David than Tom Hanks. But I've read enough about gratitude to know that it's one of the keys to a life well lived. Perhaps even, as Cicero says, it is the chief of virtues.

According to the research, gratitude's psychological benefits are legion: It can lift depression, help you sleep, improve your diet, and make you more likely to exercise. Heart patients recover more quickly when they keep a gratitude journal. A recent study showed gratitude causes people to be more generous and kinder to strangers.

Another study summarized in *Scientific American* finds that gratitude is the single best predictor of well-being and good relationships, beating out twenty-four other impressive traits such as hope, love, and creativity. As the Benedictine monk David Steindl-Rast says, "Happiness does not lead to gratitude. Gratitude leads to happiness."

So intellectually, I've long known gratitude was invaluable. And for a while now I've made modest efforts to kick-start my gratitude whenever I could—and to instill the value in my kids.

My three boys are required to write old-fashioned handwritten thank-you notes when they get birthday gifts, much to their disbelief.

When I'm running errands with my sons, I nudge them to thank the bus driver.

I even tell them they should thank our household robot Alexa when she informs us about the weather.

"Alexa doesn't have feelings," my son Jasper will say.

"Yeah, but it's good practice," I respond.

And sometimes, before a meal, I'll say a prayer of thanks-giving. Sort of. We're not a particularly religious family. I'm agnostic, verging on atheist, so instead of thanking God, I'll occasionally start a meal by thanking a handful of people who helped get our food to the plate. I'll say, "Thank you to the farmer who grew the carrots, to the truck driver who hauled them, to the cashier at Gristedes grocery store who rang me up."

"You know these people can't hear you, right?" my son Zane asked me one night.

I told him I knew, but that it's still good to remind ourselves of others' contributions.

Yet Zane's comment stayed with me. He's right. Those people can't hear me. My pre-meal thanks are kind of perfunctory.

As I pondered this over the next few days, I wondered if I should commit more fully. What would it be like to personally thank those who helped make my food? Each one of them?

I knew the idea was absurd on one level. It'd be a major headache. It'd be time-consuming and travel-heavy.

But it could also have huge benefits. It might be a nice thing for the people who make my meals possible.

It would show my sons I'm serious about gratitude, and that they should be too.

And it might make me more grateful, which would, in turn, make me less petty and annoyed. Because I needed to be less annoyed. Even though I know that I'm ridiculously lucky—I don't lack for meals and I have a job that I mostly enjoy—I still let all the daily irritations hijack my brain. I'll step on our dog's dinosaur-shaped chew toy, or I'll open an email that begins, "Dearest A.J., I regret to inform you . . . ," and I'll forget the hundreds of things that go right every day and focus on the three or four that go wrong. I'd estimate that in my default mode, I'm mildly to severely aggravated more than 50 percent of my waking hours. That's a ridiculous way to go through life. I don't want to get to heaven (if such a thing exists) and spend my time complaining about the volume of the harp music.

I'm not too far from the norm. If you believe evolutionary psychologists, all humans are genetically programmed to pay attention to what goes wrong. In Paleolithic times, it had survival value. Your one-thousandth great-grandparents needed to be damn sure they remembered which mushroom was poisonous.

But the result of this negative bias is that we are awash in modern-day anxiety. We often see our lives as problem after problem, crisis after crisis. Many of us live in what some psychologists call the "deficit" mind-set, not the "surplus" mind-set. We spend far too much time fretting about what we're missing instead of focusing on what we have.

I needed a mental makeover, and a gratitude project could be my key to success. My goal for this project was to flip my ratio: By the end, I wanted to spend more than half of my average day experiencing gratitude and mild happiness. Or at least not outright irritation.

My first task: I had to choose what food item to be thankful for. I considered apples, white wine, and Monterey Jack cheese. (My sons lobbied for s'mores, since they figured it would increase general s'more consumption around the house.)

I thought about nonfood items as well: my pen, my socks, my toothpaste. Almost every object I encounter in my day requires thousands of humans and tons of effort—effort I take totally for granted.

Finally I settled on something I can't live without. My coffee. It seemed right for a couple of reasons. First, I do love my morning cup from my local café. I take it to go, no milk. I'm not a fanatic and my palate is unrefined, but I relish coffee's bitter taste and the pleasant buzz it gives me—it's my favorite narcotic, hands down.

Second, coffee has a huge impact on our world. More than two billion cups of coffee are drunk every day around the globe. The coffee industry employs 125 million people internationally. Coffee is intertwined with politics, economics, and history. The Enlightenment was born in Europe's coffeehouses. Over the centuries, coffee has helped create international trade and shape our modern economy.

So I set out on the Great Coffee Gratitude Trail, intent on following all its twists and turns. What follows is the tale of my attempt. Oh, and lest I forget: Thank you for reading this intro.

1 The Barista and the Taster

Thanks for Serving Me My Coffee

I've decided to do this project in reverse, starting with my local café and working my way backward to the birth of the coffee. My coffee shop is a block's walk from my apartment. It's called Joe Coffee and has survived for twelve years, despite two Starbucks within a three-block radius.

On a Thursday morning, I get in line, prepping myself to say the very first "thank you" of Project Gratitude. While waiting, I force myself to stash my smartphone in my pocket and actually notice my surroundings. The act of noticing, after all, is a crucial part of gratitude; you can't be grateful if your attention is scattered.

On the wall, there's a photo of a pink Cadillac that, for some reason, is perched on top of a tower. There are moms pushing strollers, dogs tied up outside, the frequent hiss of the espresso machine. Glowing indigo lamps the shape of doughnuts hang from the ceiling. That indigo light is lovely, I think to myself. You don't see enough indigo lamps.

I get to the counter and am greeted by my barista, a twenty-something woman with hair gathered in a ponytail atop her head. She hands me my order—a small black coffee, the daily blend.

"Thank you for my coffee," I say.

"You're welcome!" she says, smiling.

And there it is. My first thank you. It's fine, but no lightning bolts yet.

I slide my credit card to pay the three-dollar fee. (Three dollars is, of course, ridiculously expensive. But in a weird sense, as I'll learn, it's also wildly underpriced.)

I hold my cup of coffee and stand there, trying to figure out what, if anything, to tell the barista about my quest. I pause five seconds too long, somewhere on the border between awkward and creepy. I glance at the line of customers behind me and slink out.

A couple of days later, I've worked up the nerve to tell the barista about Project Gratitude. I asked her if she'd be willing to share with me a bit about what goes into making my coffee. She said she'd be happy to talk after her shift.

"Thanks again for the coffee," I say, as we sit down at one of Joe's small tables.

"Thanks for thanking me," she says.

I consider thanking her for thanking me for thanking her, but decide to cut it off lest we get caught in an infinite loop.

She tells me her name is Chung. Her parents are Korean immigrants, and she grew up in Southern California before moving to New York for college.

"So . . . ," I say. "Um . . . What's it's like being a barista?"

"It's not always easy," she says. This is because you're dealing with people in a very dangerous condition: Pre-caffeination.

"You get some grouchy people?" I asked.

"Oh, they can be grumpy."

Chung tells me tales of customers who refuse to even make eye contact. They just snarl their order and thrust out their credit card, never looking up from their smartphone.

She's had customers berate her till she cried for mixing up orders (which she swears she didn't). She's been snapped at by a bratty nine-year-old girl who didn't like the milk-foam design that Chung created on top of her hot chocolate. Chung made a teddy bear. The girl wanted a heart. "I wanted to tell her that she did need a heart—a real one."

And yet, Chung says the cranky customers are the minority. Most folks are friendly, especially when Chung sets the mood by being friendly first. And man, Chung is *friendly*.

She is a smiler and a hugger. She's like a morning-show host, but not forced or fake. To give you a sense: During our half-hour chat, Chung got up no fewer than five times to hug longtime customers and former coworkers.

"I first realized I might be good at customer service when I was working as an usher at my church," she says. "I saw that it takes a certain personality."

And like at church, when she's at Joe Coffee, she sometimes watches as people are transformed, their faces lighting up when they get their cups. "I see my job as getting them coffee, but also making them happy."

I ask her if she's planning on being a barista for the long haul.

She shakes her head. "Actually, this is my last week."

She's moving back to California to take care of her parents. Plus, nowadays, she's having trouble staying up on her feet her entire shift.

"Let me give you a visual of why," Chung says.

She takes out her smartphone and swipes to a photo. It's a startling image of her left foot, bloody, bruised, and with more than a dozen metal pins sticking out of it.

"A year and a half ago, I got hit by a bus," she says. "I broke every toe, the heel, the ankle. The skin was gone."

"Oh my God."

"Yeah, it wasn't pretty."

Chung says it'll be sad to leave the regulars. She talks about Nancy and John, who arrive every morning as soon as the glass door is unlocked. "I always say, 'How's your day going?' And John will say, '*Now* it's going well.'"

She'll miss her coworkers, whom she says always have her back.

She won't miss the occasional feeling that she doesn't exist at all. "What's upsetting is when people treat us like machines, not humans," Chung says. "When they look at us as just a means to an end—or don't even look at us at all."

I thank Chung, and she gives me a hug (her eleventh of the day, by my estimate).

On my way home, I make a pledge. Though I probably won't hug any other baristas, I promise to look them in the eyes—because I know I've been that asshole who thrusts out the credit card without glancing up. I'm not sure if I ever did it to Chung, but I know I've treated many others—waiters, delivery people, bodega cashiers—as if they were vending machines. I sometimes wear these noise-cancelling headphones when running errands, so that just makes me look more aloof and unfriendly.

And this is an enemy of gratitude. UC Davis psychology professor Robert Emmons—who is considered the father of gratitude research—puts it this way: "Grateful living is possible only when we realize that other people and agents do things for us that we cannot do for ourselves. Gratitude emerges from two stages of information processing—affirmation and recognition. We affirm the good and credit others with bringing it about. In gratitude, we recognize that the source of goodness is outside of ourselves."

From now on, when I have an interaction with anyone else, I'll try to affirm and recognize them. I'll try to remember to treat them as humans—at least until robots take over all service jobs. I'll try to keep in mind that they have families and favorite movies and embarrassing teenage memories and possibly aching feet.

•   •   •

Chung served me my coffee—but who chose what type of coffee I drank? Who selected my daily blend from the tens of thousands of varieties across the globe? The answer to that takes me one step back on the chain to a man named Ed Kaufmann, head of buying at Joe Coffee Company, which now has nineteen stores in New York and Philadelphia.

Ed agrees to meet me at the Joe Coffee Company headquarters in Chelsea. He ushers me into a back room with a round table.

"Thanks for my coffee this morning," I say, making sure to look Ed in the eyes. I tell him I'd picked up a cup earlier at the Joe Coffee near my apartment and drank it on the way down.

"Did you like it?"

"Yes."

"What did you like about it?"

"Well, it woke me up. And it tasted good. Bitter, I guess? I don't have a very sophisticated palate."

"We'll work on that," he says.

Ed looks a bit like a young Elvis Costello, spectacles and all. He grew up in Montana, where his parents owned a restaurant at a ski resort. It's there that Ed first fell for coffee. "As a teenager, my friends and I would get caffeinated up and go snowboarding."

He can't snowboard here in New York, but Ed tells me he still likes the bracing cold.

He's a fan of ice baths, which he says give him energy. And every morning, even on seventeen-degree January days, he jolts himself awake by biking to work without a shirt. "Actually, now I wear a T-shirt," Ed says. "I was getting too many stares when I went shirtless."

But Ed's true love is coffee. He's smitten with it, head over heels. Some proof? He spent his honeymoon taking a five-day coffee-tasting course in Massachusetts. On his days off, he goes café hopping and "gets wasted on espresso." He talks about particular cups of coffee the way some people talk about long-lost girlfriends. "That was a meaningful cup of coffee," he'll say, about a cup he drank in Ecuador. He describes coffee with elaborate metaphors, sort of like an antic sommelier. "There was this one coffee—I call it the Wonka Coffee because it was like an Everlasting Gobstopper, flavor after flavor, just exploding."

It's only been a few minutes, but I'm grateful that Ed is so passionate about this brown liquid. I may not fully appreciate the subtleties, but on some level, I know that Ed's wisdom in choosing the best beans benefits me. The very fact that Ed thinks so deeply about my coffee is part of the reason I don't have to think about it at all. It's a key reason gratitude is so difficult to maintain, and why it takes so much effort and intention: If something is done well for us, the process behind it is largely invisible.

On the table are seven brown paper bags, each labeled with a number. Ed doesn't want to know where the coffees are from until after the tasting. He wants to be unbiased. The coffees come in from all over the world—Colombia, Ghana, the Dominican Republic, Papua New Guinea.

"Okay," he says, "here's how you do it."

Ed dips a spoon into one of the many coffee-filled white cups on the table and slurps the liquid. It's a comically loud slurp, like the slurp of an Adam Sandler character sipping soup at a fancy French restaurant.

"You have to aerate the coffee so that it sprays all over the mouth," he says. "There are taste buds everywhere—in your cheeks, even the roof of the mouth."

I try slurping a spoonful myself, but my slurp isn't nearly as loud—it's more of a piccolo to his tuba.

Ed swishes the coffee around his mouth, then spits it into a black chewing-tobacco spittoon.

"What did you think?" he asks me.

"Pretty good. Maybe a little acidic?" I say, guessing.

Ed nods his head. "I tasted some citrus, but also notes of honey." He's carrying a Moleskine notebook and scribbles some words in it.

If Ed likes any of the coffees that we're tasting, he might give them a much-coveted spot on the menu of the Joe Coffee chain. It's a small but growing chain with a hipster vibe; it has lots of bearded baristas and socially conscious symbolism. The chain pays its farmers higher than fair trade prices. It markets itself as transparent, and you can often see a sign on the counter about the featured farm of the day.

I ask Ed if I can see the words he wrote down, and he shows me some. They are delightfully, hilariously specific: graham cracker, mandarin orange, pineapple upside-down cake.

Ed will describe a coffee as having notes of apple. But not just a generic apple. He'll say, "This reminds me of a Pink Lady apple, or maybe Gala.

"I'm a sucker for baked peach and maple," he tells me. "If I see that in my notes, I know I have a winner."

Tasters like Ed are looking for several variables: mouth feel, a balance between acidity and fruitiness, aftertaste.

"You also want to avoid coffee that's too vegetal or leathery," Ed tells me.

"You don't like leather?" I ask.

"Only on weekends," he says, laughing. "I'm kidding."

Like many coffee obsessives, Ed thinks Starbucks over-roasts its coffee. It's too bitter. You can't taste the fruitiness. "I only go to Starbucks in a coffee emergency," he says.

Ed knows that not everyone is infatuated with the subtle flavors of coffee. He started as a barista at a coffee shop that was even more artisanal than Joe Coffee.

"People would come in and say, 'I'd like a cup of coffee.' And I'd say, 'Okay, what are you looking for? What flavor notes are you interested in?' And they'd say, 'I don't care. I just want my fucking cup of coffee.'"

I understand that mind-set. Sometimes you just want the fucking coffee.

But I make a promise: I'm going to try to appreciate the flavors more. It only seems fair. Consider all the thousands of hours of attention that Ed and others around the world put into each cup of coffee—and yet, every morning, I guzzle it like a dog at a bowl.

It reminds me of a conversation I had when I started Project Gratitude. I'd called up author and researcher Scott Barry Kaufman (no relation to Ed), who taught a popular course on positive psychology and gratitude at the University of Pennsylvania. I wanted a little background on the science of thankfulness.

"Gratitude has a lot to do with holding on to a moment as strongly as possible," Scott told me. "It's closely related to mindfulness and savoring. Gratitude can shift our perception of time and slow it down. It can make our life's petty annoyances dissolve away, at least for a moment."

The point is, it's hard to be grateful if we're speeding through life, focusing on what's next, as I tend to do. We need to be aware of what's in front of us. We need to stop and smell the roses, along with the graham crackers and soil and leather.

So today, while sipping coffee with Ed, I tried to practice what psychologists call *savoring meditation*. I let the coffee sit on my tongue for twenty seconds, which may not sound like a long time, but I don't want to keep Ed waiting. (And twenty seconds can be powerful if you really make each second count. Quality over quantity, right?)

I focused on the viscosity of the liquid, the acidity, the bitterness . . . Was that apricot? I still couldn't taste the distinct flavors, but I could see a way to unraveling the threads.

•   •   •

Ed and I sampled the seven coffees, sipping each of them three times—while hot, while warm, and while tepid. Different temperatures reveal different tastes.

At the end, Ed says there are no superstars in the bunch. He feels the best contender is a coffee from Burundi that scored an 85 on a scale of 100.

But it wasn't a waste of time. You never know where the next great coffee might come from, so Ed tastes anything sent to him. "People will send me a note saying, 'This is from my grandmother's farm in the Dominican Republic.'" A couple of years ago, he was sent coffee with a note that said, "This coffee has been through war zones in Yemen and you can't even taste the gunpowder." Last year, Ed tells me, he was expecting a shipment of coffee from Papua New Guinea, but it never came because tribal warfare interfered with the harvesting.

Ed goes on an international trip every year to meet with farmers—to build rapport, sample coffee, and make deals.

"I'm going to South America in a few weeks," he says. "You should come!"

He tells me that Joe's house blend—which is what I order every day—contains beans from a small family farm in Colombia. He'll be visiting that farm, and I can tag along.

"You're serious?"

"Yeah, I mean, it's not easy to get to. A flight, another flight, and then a four-hour drive. But you're invited."

And just like that, I'm going to another continent.

• • •

After the tasting, Ed and I head out for burritos near his office.

"It's kind of odd that you're featuring me in your book,"

he says, as we sit down. "Because I'm usually more of a background guy. I'm a bassist."

He means that literally. Ed plays bass guitar in a band called Erostratus, an alt rock group that sings songs about heartbreak and alcohol . . . "The usual," as Ed says.

"I like being the bassist," he says. "Everyone wants to be the lead guitarist or lead singer, and we need those. But we also need bassists. I'm necessary, but I'm background."

On my subway ride home, I can't stop thinking about Ed and his humble but essential bass guitar. It's a wonderful metaphor for my project.

In our society, we fetishize the lead singers. And not just in music. The front people in every field—art, engineering, sports, food—get way too much attention. The cult of celebrity has spread into every corner. We overemphasize individual achievement when, in fact, almost everything good in the world is the result of teamwork. Consider the polio vaccine, which qualifies as a very good thing. According to the book *Give and Take*, by psychologist Adam Grant, Jonas Salk took all the glory for inventing the polio vaccine. He was on the cover of *Time*; he became the household name.

But the truth of the vaccine's invention is more nuanced. Salk was part of a team at the University of Pittsburgh. There were six researchers who made major contributions, not to mention three scientists who figured out how to grow polio in test tubes, a crucial advance that made the vaccine possible. In other words, there were many bassists who helped conquer polio. And they were overlooked, which they rightly felt bitter about. In a 1955 press conference about the vaccine, Salk neglected to thank his collaborators. Many of them left the conference in tears.

Psychologists have a name for this failure to acknowledge and thank collaborators: the "responsibility bias." For one thing, it causes a lot of pain and resentment among the billions of unacknowledged bass players in our world.

But its long-term consequences might be even worse. By elevating individual achievement over cooperation, we're creating a glut of wannabe superstars who don't have time for collaboration. We desperately need more bassists in the world. We can see this playing out in many industries, but let me stick with science for a second. Your typical scientist craves the glory of creating a bold new hypothesis, instead of the equally important but less flashy task of replicating experiments to make sure the conclusions are true. This has led to what's called the "replication crisis." A shocking amount of our scientific knowledge may be inaccurate because we don't have enough bassists in lab coats doing backup.

I'm not immune to the responsibility bias. This book has my name on the cover, but its existence is the work of dozens of people. The idea of a lone author warps reality. In a more accurate world, this book would have many names on the cover, not just mine. We considered it, but my editor, Michelle Quint—one of the best bassists in publishing—thought such a cover would be too confusing and hard to read, so here I am, perpetuating the lead singer myth.

At the very least, I can do what Emmons says is the core of gratitude: affirm and recognize what I didn't do myself. So thank you to the cover designer, the marketers, the freelance researchers, the printing plant workers, the sawmill operators . . . as you can see, this could be its own book.

2 The Cup Makers

Thanks for Stopping the Coffee from Spilling on My Lap

It's a week after my talk with Ed, and it hasn't been a fun morning.

I spent a frustrating three minutes trying to wrestle my contact lenses onto my eyeballs, which seemed determined to repel them.

I grabbed an aluminum water bottle for the road, but then wasted another two minutes trying to find the proper cap. I have at least seven caps of different shapes and sizes, and I failed the impromptu IQ test of finding the correct one.

A bit later, I stepped onto the subway platform just in time to see a C train pull away into the dark tunnel.

They're little things, I know. They're problems of a decidedly first-world nature. But they came one after another, and the accumulation has pushed up my cortisol level. My annoyance ratio for the day is already well above 90 percent.

Since I'm doing a project on gratitude, I figure I'd better practice some thankfulness to try to calm myself down. So as I stand on the platform, I remind myself of this fact: Just as hundreds of things must go right for my coffee to exist, I've also had hundreds of things go right for me today.

For starters:

I did not trip on the subway stairs and break my collarbone.

The elevator in my building did not plummet to the basement and give me a concussion.

My fare card had enough money on it to get me through the turnstile, which didn't stick when I pushed it.

The key is to remind myself that I'm a lucky bastard. To make a concerted effort to acknowledge all the good things I take for granted. To battle my brain's built-in negative bias, the one that might have helped our Paleo ancestors avoid predators but that often puts me in a miserable mood.

Yes, I missed the train today, but what about all the times I got to the subway platform just as the doors were opening, allowing me to slip into the car while suppressing a smug smile? The reality is, I'm not unlucky with subways—it just seems that way because the enraging experiences are the ones that stick in my memory. It's the same distorted way that I process feedback. If I get one hundred compliments and one insult, what do I remember? The insult.

Fighting this bias requires an active strategy. A commitment to noticing. The next time I'm in a drugstore line that moves quickly, or am assigned an airport gate located right next to security instead of a half-mile walk past frozen yogurt shops, I vow to actually point out my good fortune to myself. I'll even say it out loud: "I'm grateful this line was so short!" Maybe that'll get it through my thick, biased skull.

I've become a fan of a mental game I call "It could be worse." It can be a creative little exercise. I think to myself: The subway signs are confusing, but at least they're in English, not Latvian. The subway platform is depressing, but at least there's no one singing "Bohemian Rhapsody" next to an open guitar case.

I recently read an article about the poet Robert Bly, who said that when he was a kid and skinned his knee, his mother would say, "Just be thankful that you didn't break your leg." He found it annoying at the time, which is understandable. But he now sees its perverse wisdom.

•   •   •

A while later, I get to the office I rent (it's the size of a closet, but I remind myself it has a door and working AC!). I flick on the lights, put my Joe Coffee cup down on my desk, and realize that if I'm going to thank everyone who has made my cup of coffee a reality, I have to thank the cup makers too. I don't drink my coffee out of the spigot.

But thanking the cup makers is no simple task. The cup has many elements. I decide to start from the top, with the lid.

The Lid

I've never paid much attention to the white plastic lid on my morning coffee. But when I inspect it, I notice that it's not an ordinary lid. It's got a funky design. It isn't flat-topped like many coffee lids. It's got depth. It looks like a chunk of an upside-down geodesic dome, like something from

Buckminster Fuller's notebook. And the sipping hole? It's almost elegant: crescent-shaped, like a quarter moon.

When I google the name on the lid —"Viora"—I discover that I'm sipping my coffee through a superstar cover. Viora is a small newcomer but has been written up in tech publications including *Wired* and *Gizmodo*. It's sort of the Tesla of the lid world.

"We are not rocket scientists. Rocket science does nothing to improve the taste of your coffee," Viora's website humbly points out.

Before contacting Viora, I spend an afternoon doing a deep dive into the world of coffee lids. I didn't know a deep dive was possible, but it is: I learn that lids can be classified into several categories, depending on how you open them—the Pinch, the Puncture, the Peel, and the Pucker. I learn about dozens of wacky patents, including a lid that changes color according to the coffee's heat. I learn that the man who patented the press-down tab is a notorious billionaire who renounced his U.S. citizenship to live in Belize, the Caribbean tax haven. And I learn that coffee lids are a huge business. Over 1 billion are sold per year.

In short, I learn that, as with almost everything I take for granted, humans have put an astounding amount of thought and care into creating this unassuming piece of plastic.

I email the inventor of the Viora lid. His name is Doug Fleming, and he's a coffee-obsessed attorney in Seattle. When he calls the next day, I explain my project.

"So . . . I just wanted to tell you, 'thank you,'" I say.

"That's good to hear," Doug says. "Lids don't get a lot of attention."

In Doug's view, this is a shame. The lid is a crucial—and wildly undervalued—part of drinking coffee.

"Coffee isn't farm to cup," he tells me. "It's farm to face. You actually have to drink it. And coffee is very delicate. Tweak just a few things in coffee and it becomes cat piss. And I think it's terrible when coffee is ruined at the end with a bad lid. It's like you walk a thousand miles and blow it on the last step."

The ideal lid, Doug says, is one that doesn't interfere with the drinking experience. You should feel like you're drinking right from an old-style ceramic cup . . . sort of how the ideal condom should feel like you're not wearing it (my analogy, not his).

But what, I ask, could really go wrong with a lid? Doug tells me the first big pitfall is the aroma. It's the problem that inspired Doug to tinker with lids in the first place. He was at a meeting with a client, sipping a cup of coffee with a lid, and noticed there was no smell. It was as if he had a stuffed nose.

Doug started doodling complicated designs for a two-chamber lid with a plastic gizmo to pump the aroma into your nose like a geyser. He eventually settled on a simpler solution: a lid with a bigger hole in the center, and with a deeper crevice to accommodate our noses.

While he's talking, I bring my coffee to my nose and take a strong sniff through the lid. Ah, that's the bitter stuff.

The second big problem is the splash. Most lids shoot the coffee upward, spouting it into your mouth. Not ideal for controlled sipping. "We wanted a lid that lets the coffee come out smoothly, like you're drinking from a mug." Doug and his partner designed a sipping hole that's carved into the inner lip of the lid. The hole isn't flat on the lid, as with most. "The mouth should be in the right position. It needs to be relaxed. Some lids make you pucker your lips like you're sucking a straw. And that means you're not getting the retronasal experience."

He pauses. "I mean, I don't want to get too geeky on you."

"That ship sailed long ago," I say. The conversation has indeed been geeky since the start, but talking to Doug, I find myself smiling, occasionally chuckling. There's unexpected joy in discovering how much brainpower has gone into this seemingly mundane object.

Doug tells me it's been a struggle. No one wanted to manufacture the oddly shaped hole. Everyone told him it couldn't be done. Finally, Doug and his partner found a company in Canada that helps produce plastic raspberry boxes, which also have weirdly shaped slits.

So they imported the tools from Canada to a factory in Tennessee, where every day buckets of special odor-free plastic pellets are melted down, rolled into sheets, sucked onto molds, peeled off, loaded into boxes, and trucked to stores like Joe Coffee.

And there it is: perfection. Or not. Doug tells me that he's not finished with revolutionizing lids. "I'm actually working on a new coffee lid now that will be my *Mona Lisa*," Doug tells me. The secret is . . . well, I'm not supposed to write about it yet. It's a cutthroat game, the lid biz.

But this I can tell you: I will not take my coffee lid for granted again. And over the next few days I try to appreciate all the other little hidden masterpieces of industrial design in my life. I'm grateful for the way the on/off switch on my lamp has a smooth indentation for my thumb. I'm grateful for the star-shaped holes in my spaghetti strainer. Small works of genius everywhere.

The Logo

The lid, of course, snaps onto a cardboard cup. I inspect the cup more closely. The surface is colored robin's-egg blue and adorned with three letters, *JOE*.

COFFEE COMPANY

I like the logo. It's simple and sleek. Since a good logo is crucial to a functioning business, I figure I should thank the designer.

The folks at Joe Coffee give me the phone number of a man named Marke Johnson who lives in Denver.

"Thank you," I say, when I call him up.

"Well, it's my job," he says. "But you're welcome."

"Can I ask you how you got the job to design the logo?"

Marke's answer is more absurdly hipster than I could have dreamed. A few years ago, Marke was in a thirteen-person band called the Cinematic Underground that crisscrossed America in a converted school bus. Marke played guitar but also designed the band's multimedia slide shows. The band's trumpet player went on to work at Joe Coffee and eventually recommended Marke for a logo redesign. And voilà.

"Who are your other clients, aside from coffee?" I ask.

"We recently got to rebrand a whiskey," he says. "And I've had tons of meetings with marijuana dispensaries."

"I'm sensing a theme."

"Yeah." He laughs. "A large part of our business comes from branding mind-altering substances and trying to make them socially acceptable."

When Marke—whose company is called the Made Shop— got the Joe Coffee Company account, he and his team flew to New York to absorb the ambience and liquid. He decided Joe Coffee had a welcoming vibe, and the logo should reflect that.

Thus began endless rounds of meetings and ideas and sketches, some good, some terrible. As with the lid, I'm awed by the amount of anguish that goes into the smallest of decisions.

Consider the choice of typeface. It took days. They wanted something Art Deco, but the usual Art Deco fonts weren't quite right. "They were too cold and sharp and not friendly enough," Marke says. They finally stumbled across a font

called Nanami whose "corners were rounded just a tiny bit."
I squint at the letter *E* on my cup and notice that, yes, the
corners look like they've been sandpapered.

Another challenge: The executives at Joe Coffee wanted the
logo to somehow contain an image of a coffee cup, but Marke
was skeptical. A coffee cup seemed too clichéd. He'd been
hoping to get away from Joe Coffee's previous logo, which had
a silhouette of one of those big old nineties mugs. "It looked
like something Rachel from *Friends* would drink from,"
Marke says.

But Marke and his team hit upon the idea of changing
the perspective. What if the image of a cup was seen from a
bird's-eye view, nestled inside the letter *O*?

There's a whole genre of secret images in logos—the famous
arrow lurking in the FedEx logo, the bear hidden in the
Toblerone logo. "Our coffee cup isn't as hidden as those. But
the hope is that it'll take a moment to notice it. That it will give
you just a little bit of a surprise."

As I'm talking to Marke on the phone, I look around my
office. I see logos all over—the red swish of my Purell bottle,
the cheery yellow lettering of my Pepto-Bismol. This is my
scenery, my landscape.

"There are logos everywhere, even when I go camping I
can't escape logos," Marke says. "A lot of designs are good
but a lot are terrible. I know a musician who has an extreme
problem with background music in malls. For me, logos are
analogous to that. It's frustrating. There's a Walgreens near

my house, and they have a poster advertising three items. And there's noticeably more space between two of the items. Every time I see it, I get furious."

I laugh. I can't imagine getting outraged by a slightly lopsided poster. I tell Marke that maybe he needs to sip some rebranded whiskey or to smoke some legally purchased pot.

And yet I'm glad Marke has that infatuation, because these logos are what I see every day. I'm grateful that he's committed to making our world just a little more elegant. And Marke has given Joe customers a nice logo: clean, friendly, less baffling than the Starbucks green mermaid wearing a crown.

Who knows? Maybe his logo even helped me enjoy my coffee more. In researching coffee, I've run across several experiments showing that external factors affect people's judgment of a coffee's taste. When the same coffee is served in a fancier cup, people think it tastes better. We are an easily manipulated species.

I thank Marke again and promise to be more appreciative of all the folks trying to make the world less ugly.

The Sleeve

I'm making cold calls to thank people for my cup and getting mixed reactions. The guy who answered the phone at a tree farmer association, whose members grow the wood used in my paper cup, responded with the same tone I use when I'm asked to take an E-Meter reading on the street.

"I know this sounds odd, but I want to thank you . . . ," I started.

"I'm good," he said.

"No, I'm not trying to sell . . . "

He'd already clicked off.

But many others were more receptive, like the woman who helped create the coffee cup sleeve, the brown cardboard ring you slip onto your coffee cup to protect you from the heat.

Again, I'd never devoted much time to thinking about the sleeve, but it's really a remarkable little invention. Consider the millions, perhaps billions, of fingers and thumbs these cardboard sleeves have saved from burning, or at least from mildly annoying pain.

A little research revealed that coffee cup sleeves have been around since ancient times. They even have a name: zarfs. Turkish coffee and Chinese tea were served to nobles in zarfs made from gold, silver, tortoiseshell, and other materials.

The modern cardboard version, though, was born in 1992 in Portland and is called the Java Jacket. Java Jacket Inc. is still around and remains a family-owned business run by Jay Sorensen and his wife, Colleen. I find the phone number and Colleen answers.

"Thank you. You've saved my fingertips so many hours of unpleasantness," I say.

"That's nice to hear," she says.

I ask Colleen to tell me the origin of the Java Jacket. It's a delightfully simple tale, as clear as the falling apple that supposedly inspired Isaac Newton. One day, Colleen's husband, Jay, got in his car to buy lunch to bring their daughter at school. He pulled up to the drive-through. He took the cup from the kid at the window—and felt his fingers start to singe. He reflexively let go. The coffee spilled in his lap, and he presumably said some words that I won't print here.

Jay went home and started brainstorming ideas with Colleen around their kitchen table, trying to figure out how to prevent this from happening again.

It was a particularly dark time in their lives, says Colleen. "We were just getting by." Jay had opened a Shell gas station with his dad, but it had recently closed. Colleen was doing odd catering jobs, and while she liked the "nice people and free food," it was barely making ends meet.

"We borrowed $10,000 from Jay's folks, made some proto-types, and sold them out of the back of our car," Colleen says. A few months later, they drove to a coffee convention, where the Java Jacket was a hit with café owners. "We collected all these names and addresses and sent off four thousand samples."

Within a couple of years, they were a profitable business and able to hire several employees. "It was like the American dream come true," Colleen says. She quit being a cater-waiter and now spends her time on Java Jacket and working with a charity that delivers leftover restaurant food to the homeless.

When I hear their story, I'm once again thrilled. It's almost Capra-esque. I'm grateful tales like Colleen's still exist. I'm grateful there's still room in America for families—and not just the R&D departments of Fortune 500 companies—to come up with a goofy but surprisingly useful idea and then turn it into a reality that makes millions of lives just an eensy bit better.

"It's been a wild ride," Colleen says. She tells me about the time she was watching TV and saw a car commercial and, to her surprise, the driver was using a Java Jacket. It was their first national exposure. "You know that feeling you get when you have a crush on someone, that little giddy feeling? That's what I felt."

A few years later, the Java Jacket got an even bigger honor. It was featured in a Museum of Modern Art exhibit called "Humble Masterpieces," where it was displayed alongside an aspirin tablet and LEGO bricks. Colleen calls the experience surreal. "I remember going to New York and it was kind of overwhelming," says Colleen. "I went to MoMA—the actual MoMA!—and there was our Java Jacket in a glass case. I remember I didn't stay in the room long, because I wanted to see the Picassos and Monets."

Before I hang up, I ask Colleen to be honest. "Are you grateful I called, or was it more of a pain in your neck?"

"No, I'm happy you called. It reminded me how lucky I am. I really feel I won the lottery. I mean, I wouldn't want everyone who uses the Java Jacket to call, since I might not get any work done. But I'm happy you called."

This is a relief. When it's effective, gratitude should be a two-way street. It should be helpful to both the thanker and the thankee. It's not just a self-help tool, it should brighten other lives. I'm sure there are Greta Garbos out there who just want to be left alone and unthanked. I have to be careful. But luckily Colleen isn't one of them.

• • •

The next day I'm feeling something besides gratitude. I'm feeling overwhelmed.

I've spent several days researching and thanking those involved in coffee cups, and I haven't even gotten to the makers of the cup itself.

When I ponder the number of gratitude recipients involved, I start to get dizzy. There are the folks at the paper factory where the cardboard is made. The lumberjacks who cut down the trees for the wood pulp to make the cardboard. The metalworkers who manufacture the chainsaws the lumberjacks use. The miners who dig up the iron that is turned into the steel for the chainsaws.

It's like a particularly vicious series of pop-up ads. Every time I identify another step, I'm confronted with hundreds of divergent paths. I could write a thousand books, depending on what corridors I venture down.

I remind myself: Don't forget the folks who make the hardhats that the miners wear when getting the iron that's turned into steel to make the chainsaws the lumberjacks use to cut down the trees to get the wood pulp to make the cup that my coffee comes in.

Deep breath.

In Paleolithic times, my project would have been much easier. But with globalization—which I do think is a force for good, despite its many pitfalls—thanking everyone involved in my cup of coffee could be a lifetime job.

Over dinner with Julie and the kids, I tell them I'm feeling snowed under. "I seriously think I might have to thank every single human on earth," I say.

Julie looks skeptical. She points to the *People* magazine lying nearby on the radiator.

"What about her? How did Beyoncé help make your coffee?"

I pause for a minute, and then I come up with an answer. With enough research, I explain, I could probably get to Beyoncé. Maybe one of the engineers who made the plastic lining for my coffee cup listened to Beyoncé songs to motivate her while studying for her chemistry final. Maybe the guy who drove the warehouse truck blasted Beyoncé to stay alert.

"That's kind of a stretch, don't you think?" Julie says.

"Yes and no," I say. We are all so interconnected; it's hard to know where to draw the line.

"What about us?" Lucas asks. "How did we help?"

After a minute, I come up with this response: Julie and I have to work to support Lucas and his brothers. And our taxes pay for the roads that the coffee is delivered on and the cops who keep Joe Coffee from being robbed.

"So, thank you," I say.

I'm sensing I might have a convert in Zane. He points out it's not just people living now who helped.

"Also, what about the parents of the woman at the coffee store?" he says. "And their parents. And their parents. And their parents."

"Right," I say, glad to have a bit of support. "It's millions of dead people too, like the guy who first forged steel, and the goatherd in ancient Ethiopia who noticed his goats started dancing after eating a particular plant, and decided to try the coffee beans himself. At least that's the legend."

If I believed in séances, I'd have to thank them too.

After dinner, on reflection, I have to admit Julie's right. Thanking Beyoncé is just too far afield. I need to limit myself. Maybe I'll just try to thank a thousand people. That can be my goal. Thanks a thousand. It's huge, but manageable.

3 The Roasters
Thanks for Taking the Heat

A few days later, as Julie gets ready for her morning walk, I look her in the eyes, and say, "I just want to let you know that I am deeply grateful that you took Lucas to the orthodontist yesterday."

"Okaaaay," she says, pulling on her boots. "You're deeply welcome, I guess."

Point taken. The phrase "deeply grateful" is a tad formal, bordering on unsettling. I sound like a member of an Oregon cult who practices nude meditation.

But I have a reason. I recently read a Wharton study that concluded that people who say the phrase "I am grateful" are seen as more genuinely thankful than when people simply say "thank you."

So I've been test-driving the "I am grateful" construction and throwing in the occasional "deeply" for emphasis.

The gist of the study is that the phrase "thank you" is too often seen as robotic, a mere verbal reflex. If you switch it up with other gratitude phrases, maybe it will jolt people awake, cause them to take notice.

So far, the responses have been varied—a lot of genuine smiles, several nervous ones. This morning I told the barista at Joe, "I'm really grateful for this coffee."

"As well you should be," he said, laughing. His confidence brightened my day.

Oddly, the biggest impact of using this phrase might be on my own psyche. When I force myself to utter the awkward phrase "I am grateful," I actually start to feel a bit more grateful.

Maybe I shouldn't be surprised. It confirms a huge theme I've noticed in my previous writing projects: That the exterior shapes the interior. That our speech and actions change our thoughts. There's a great quote from the man who founded Habitat for Humanity that describes this phenomenon. He said: "It's easier to act your way into a new way of thinking than to think your way into a new way of acting."

Let me give you a quick example. A few years ago, I wrote a book in which I decided to give myself a crash course in religion. I tried to learn about the Bible by living it, by following all the biblical rules as literally as possible. I attempted to abide by the Ten Commandments. I grew a bushy Moses-like beard. I avoided wearing clothes made of mixed fibers (as instructed by Leviticus).

I also had to try to become more compassionate, which is not my natural state. How could I make this happen? My strategy was to force myself to act *as if* I were compassionate.

At the time I had a friend in the hospital. I hate hospitals. I hate everything about them, including the smell, which manages to be simultaneously antiseptic and putrid. But I said to myself, "What would a compassionate person do? He or she would visit the friend in the hospital." And so I forced myself to go.

When I got to the hospital, a strange thing happened. I tricked my brain. My brain said, "Look, I'm in the hospital visiting my friend. I must be a compassionate person!" If you do this often enough, you become a bit more compassionate for real. It's basic cognitive behavioral therapy: Behave in a certain way, and your mind will eventually catch up to your actions.

The same fake-it-till-you-make-it phenomenon happened when I wrote an article about trying to be the best husband I could be. Every day, I forced myself to buy a little gift for Julie—marzipan, magnets, overpriced soap that smelled of guava.

Once again, I outsmarted my brain. My brain thought: "I'm buying my wife these trinkets, I must really love her." And my love got a little stronger.

I'm seeing a similar shift with gratitude. I'm expressing gratitude out loud enough times that my mind is catching up. I'm still far from my goal to be annoyed less than half the time, but it's a start.

Later that morning, I head off to Brooklyn to say "I'm grateful" to some folks there. Ed Kaufmann has invited me to the Joe Coffee roastery. This is the place where the raw green coffee beans are shipped from around the world, cooked dark brown, and put into vans to deliver to the cafés.

The facility is a cavernous space with brick walls, wood beams, forklifts, cardboard boxes, and an incongruous golden chandelier hanging from the ceiling.

"Welcome to our kitchen," Ed greets me.

The most noticeable part of the roastery is, not surprisingly, the roasters. These are huge steel machines that look, in Ed's words, "like a pizza oven and a clothes dryer had a baby."

They each have an enormous steel bucket filled with coffee beans, a metallic arm stirring them, and a roaring gas-powered fire underneath. Next to the roaster is a computer screen with a colorful Dow Jones–like graph.

"That's to keep track of the temperature inside the roaster," Ed explains.

You don't just turn the roaster to 350 degrees and go do the crossword, he explains. Every minute of the twelve-minute roasting cycle must be at a different temperature to produce the ideal coffee. You need someone adjusting the dials, an employee monitoring it second by second.

The roasting oven is just one of dozens of gadgets. I look around, and the place resembles a nonviolent version of Q's lab in a Bond movie.

There's a toaster-size appliance that makes a whirring noise and then displays your beans' moisture level (11 percent is good). There's another piece of equipment that looks like a thermometer. It measures stability, meaning how much the coffee beans' chemistry might change.

"When I was in Colombia, the farmers roasted a cup of coffee in a frying pan, and it was so good," Ed says. "So it can be done without all this stuff. But we don't like to take chances."

The roasting facility has more than machines. There are still several people working here, at least until the artificial intelligence revolution comes.

Ed introduces me to Eric, who has on a bicycle cap and a T-shirt with sleeves rolled up to his shoulders. "It can get hot in here," Eric explains.

Eric is one of a team of five men in charge of loading, weighing, and bagging the coffee.

"I just want to say I'm grateful to you for helping make my cup of coffee," I say.

"Thanks, man," Eric responds. "I drink it too, so I know it can make or break a day."

Eric explains that each member of the team has his own method for schlepping the 152-pound burlap bags of coffee beans as they come off the trucks. One guy ties "three or four together with an orange strap and pulls them like a mule." Eric prefers to slide them across the floor, "like a bar drink."

"We were thinking of opening a CrossFit here," one of the men says. "We could charge people $100 an hour to move the bags."

After the beans are roasted, Eric and his colleagues use oversize steel scoopers to shovel them into five-pound bags.

"I like to finish a bag, fold it up, and then go on to the next one," says Eric's colleague Lee. "But Eric is the artist. He'll do three massive scoops in ten different bags, then finish them all off with a drizzle, so it's exactly five pounds."

I ask if I can take a thank-you photo, since I'm making an album of all the thankees. Four of the guys—including Eric and Lee—say yes. But there's another long-haired man sitting on a forklift. He waves me off. He's not interested in being thanked. I'm not sure why. Maybe he thinks it's condescending to be thanked. Maybe he just wants to be left alone to do his job. Maybe the other guys do as well but are too polite to say so.

•   •   •

That weekend Julie and I take the kids on a trip to visit our friends Ruti and Andrew in Rhode Island. Ruti is an international relations professor at Providence College. I tell her about Project Gratitude.

"Are you serious?" she asks. "You know I just taught a course in the economics of coffee?"

I did not know that. I don't believe in fate, but I can still be grateful for life's little serendipities, and this is a wonderful one. Ruti spends the weekend talking to me about the supply chain.

"One thing to remember: Don't whitewash the process," she says. "Some of these plantations are barely better than slave labor."

I tell her I'll be careful. I say that I buy from Joe Coffee, a company that seems to have a good social conscience.

"That may be true. But just keep in mind there's a lot of oppression on the path that coffee takes."

Ruti's right. I don't want to be Pollyanna-ish about this complicated issue. Coffee causes much good in the world, but it also causes massive suffering. In fact, I've been keeping a list of the beverage's pros and cons on my computer.

On the good side,

- Drinking coffee delivers little bursts of dopamine to millions of people every day. It has provided the fuel for many great works of art and engineering. Beethoven famously had a cup every morning (exactly sixty-four beans), and Balzac downed an alarming fifty cups each day.

- Coffee is an enormous economic engine for prosperity. Coffee provides jobs for an estimated 125 million people worldwide. In the words of Mark Pendergrast in his book *Uncommon Grounds*, coffee is "an essential cash crop for struggling family farmers, the basis for national industrialization and modernization [and] a model of organic production and fair trade."

- Coffee even helped the North win the Civil War. At least that's my theory. The Union had real coffee, but because of the naval blockade, the South had to make do with caffeine-free substitutes made of chicory, corn, and other substances. So I credit coffee with saving our nation.

On the bad side,

- Coffee can wreak havoc on the environment. A group called ClimatePath estimates that one pound of coffee—growing, packaging, shipping, etc.—creates five pounds of carbon dioxide. And that's not to mention the billions of discarded plastic coffee lids floating in the Pacific. Or how coffee plantations are wiping out forests in Central America.

- Coffee is the stimulant of choice by employers who want to overwork their laborers for an unhealthy number of hours.

- Coffee farming has led to vast wealth imbalances, with a lucky handful making fortunes as millions remain mired in poverty. Again, to quote *Uncommon Grounds*, coffee has "led to the oppression and land dispossession of indigenous peoples, the abandoning of subsistence agriculture in favor of exports [and] overreliance on foreign markets."

So Ruti has a point. My project can't all be happy and shiny. I have to confront coffee's harsh side as well. I can't let gratitude devolve into its unhelpful cousin, complacency. I don't want to be so thankful that I start to believe the world is perfect.

Which some people argue is the greatest danger of gratitude. Author Barbara Ehrenreich wrote a *New York Times* op-ed a few years ago called "The Selfish Side of Gratitude." In the piece, she says that gratitude can be the enemy of positive social change.

She sees gratitude as an opiate of the people. Walmart employees are told to embrace gratitude instead of complain about their low pay. Ehrenreich even hints that the gratitude movement is a right-wing plot. "Perhaps it's no surprise that gratitude's rise to self-help celebrity status owes a lot to the conservative-leaning John Templeton Foundation," she writes. "At the start of this decade, the foundation, which promotes free-market capitalism, gave $5.6 million to Dr. Emmons, the gratitude researcher."

The op-ed is worrisome. Could it be that I'm simply a dupe? I call my gratitude guru Scott Barry Kaufman and pose the question to him.

"It's an interesting claim, but empirically it just doesn't check out," Scott says, to my great relief. "Actually, it's the opposite. Research shows that people are more generous and pro-social when they feel gratitude."

Scott refers me to one such study showing that gratitude inspires people to pay it forward. It's an ingenious experiment. The psychologists—including David DeSteno from Northeastern University—brought two volunteers to a lab, sat them at adjoining cubicles, and asked each to do a boring computer task.

After twenty minutes, Subject A's computer crashed and wiped out all the progress. Subject A would have to start over and waste another twenty minutes. It was exasperating.

At which point, Subject B offered to help fix the computer. But here's the twist: Subject B was actually an insider, a confederate. The computer was rigged to crash, and Subject B simply had to press a secret button to "fix" the computer.

After the computer fix, Subject A was free to go, presumably filled with gratitude. But here's the final twist. As Subject A was leaving the building he or she was asked by another stranger for help with an unrelated task. And guess what? Subject A was much more likely to help the stranger than a control group who never went through the computer "crash," and never received help from Subject B. That was the big finding: Grateful people volunteered to help far more often. They paid it forward.

When I read the study, I send a thank-you note to Scott. This is heartening. My more cynical side had long thought gratitude likely evolved for selfish reasons. It probably began as a version of indebtedness, tit for tat: If Chimp A picks lice off Chimp B, then Chimp B is more likely to share food with Chimp A.

This is fine as far as it goes; there's nothing wrong with reciprocity. But these studies indicated that gratitude may have outgrown its realpolitik origins. It's expanded beyond returning favors and boosted our menschiness level toward strangers.

I've experienced this myself. I know I'm just one data point, but when I'm feeling grateful, I'm happier, and more likely to think of others. I'm more likely to empathize, to volunteer, to donate money to good causes. When I'm cranky or depressed, I revert to the selfish mind-set. "My life is miserable, so why should I bother helping anyone else?"

So that's a goal for this project. Avoid complacency. Make certain that gratitude is a spark for action, a way to actually improve the lives of the people along the chain even just a tiny bit. How to improve them? I don't have an answer for that yet.

4 The Water
Thanks for Filling My Cup

I've been trying to implement some of the strategies I read in books about gratitude. The psychologist Emmons suggests: "Next time you are feeling grateful to someone, give him or her a hug, or a touch on the hand or shoulder."

In this post–Harvey Weinstein world, unsolicited hugs seem like an excellent strategy to avoid.

But another strategy seems safer: Writing thank-you notes. I carve out an hour around lunchtime every day and write about ten notes that I send off via email, LinkedIn, and good old-fashioned paper envelopes. The etiquette books say the more personal the better, so I try to add details, like thanking the nonprofit worker at the Coffee Quality Institute (which advises farmers on better techniques) for heading out into the field and putting up with the mosquitos. Most of the people don't write back, which I remind myself is fine. I shouldn't expect a thank you for my thank you. But when I do get a note back, I'm thrilled. It's like an espresso buzz times ten.

Today I got an email from an engineer at GrainPro, which makes a specialty plastic bag that keeps the beans fresh during shipping. He wrote a couple of paragraphs, ending with "on behalf of my proud colleagues in GrainPro, I thank you for your great comments that have made us joyous." *Joyous* no less!

I write enough thank-you notes that I decide to make a trip to the post office for new stamps. And while I'm there, maybe I can thank the postal workers for delivering mail to Joe Coffee. I check the Internet to find out the hours. In the corner, I spot a link for the Yelp page of my local post office. I click on it. It did not fare well. A lot of one-star reviews. "This place will drain any happiness from you," writes a woman named Anna. Someone named Chin calls the employees not just grumpy but full-on "sadistic." Sam says it's a "great destination if your time is worthless."

But one reviewer named Biff Buffalo has a different perspective. He writes, "Treat the employees with kindness and they will treat you the same way back. I give them cookies several times a year."

I am in awe of Biff. His gesture is at once lovely and completely insane. But it fits into my gratitude project. Later that day, I buy a bag of Hershey bars (I figure homemade cookies might be rejected as dangerous), and bring them with me on my post-office trip.

When I get to the front of the line, the postal worker calls out "Next!"

"I'm trying to be more grateful," I say, when I walk up. "And I know you work hard, so I thought I'd bring you a thank-you gift for you to share with the staff here."

"Oh man," he says.

He lifts the window barrier and I put the bag on the scale.

"I mean, I don't want you to think I'm bribing you as a government employee. I just wanted to give you a little thank you."

"Oh man," he says again, laughing.

I can't tell if "Oh man" means "Oh man, please don't be packing a rifle," or "Oh man, what a lovely unexpected kindness."

He gives me my stamps quickly and efficiently, without sadism. My happiness is not drained.

After the post office, I head to Joe to get my coffee. As I'm sipping it, I think back to something Ed told me. Coffee is just a small part of coffee. The ratio in my cup is 1.2 percent crushed beans, 98.8 percent water. So if I'm going to thank everyone involved in my cup of coffee, I better thank those who provide the vast majority of the liquid.

For research, I read a book about the history of drinking water and am reminded how amazing it is that we can twist a little knob and immediately have a gush of clean, safe water.

This has not been the case for 99 percent of human history. And it's still not true in much of the world, where a depressingly large portion of many people's days are spent walking to wells, bucket in hand. As James Salzman writes in *Drinking Water*, millions of African women make daily trips that "squeeze out their opportunities for employment or education, perpetuating gender inequality and poverty."

But my family is absurdly lucky enough to live in a place where, within seconds, we can access water for our coffee, our showers, and our pet tortoise's daily spritz-down. And in New York, we don't get just any water. New York water has the deserved reputation of being the "champagne of waters"—clean and tasty, sometimes even bottled and sold in Europe as a novelty item.

A few days later, I'm ninety-nine miles north of Manhattan in a small town in the Catskill Mountains called Kingston. I'm on a hike with a man named Adam Bosch, a former local newspaper reporter who now works for the Department of Environmental Protection.

We're gazing out at a vast blue lake, the wind whipping the water into whitecaps. "It's not hyperbole to say that New York City would literally not exist without this water," Adam says.

Somewhere in that lake are the drops of water that, over the next several months, will travel down miles of tubes, get sprayed with chlorine, zapped with ultraviolet light, and eventually climb the pipes of Joe Coffee's sink and land in my cup.

The first thing that strikes me is the size of the lake. I can barely see the other shore. And this lake is just one of many. New York City is supplied by a collection of nineteen reservoirs. Together, they cover an area nearly twice the size of Rhode Island. We're talking 580 billion gallons of water. In one day alone, New York City consumes enough water to fill ten Yankee Stadiums.

The second thing that strikes me is how much it looks like an ordinary lake. I somehow expected New York's water to be protected by forty-foot-tall barbed wire and sniper towers to rival those overlooking the 1960s Berlin Wall. But no. Up here, it's relatively open.

It's more like a public park. A woman in a purple bandana rides her bicycle by us, singing loudly. The shore is dotted with white-hulled motorboats that cruise around in New York's future drinking water.

"There's really good fishing here," says Adam. "They caught a state-record walleye here a few years ago."

Huh. My drinking water is shared with fish. I hadn't thought about it. It's a bit jarring, at least to me—and also, apparently, to the hundreds of school kids who visit every year.

"When we get school tours, the kids always ask about fish poop," Adam says.

"And?" I say.

Adam tells the kids it's not an issue. There's just so much water, it practically disappears, he explains.

It's not just fish. Beavers, deer, and geese all make their homes in and around the reservoir. The DEP works to minimize their effects. "We set off fireworks to scare off the geese—but you can't get all of them," Adam says. Before a big rainstorm, DEP employees walk along the banks, picking up deer and mouse droppings. Those folks deserve some serious thanks.

A white pickup truck pulls up. Out steps Mark Dubois—a mustachioed man wearing sunglasses. He's one of the monitors of the reservoirs, and his family's been in the area for generations.

"My great-grandfather's house was right over there," Mark says, pointing at a spot in the middle of the lake. "It's now under about fifty feet of water."

Yes, Mark's ancestor's house was swallowed up by the reservoir. Back in 1905, there were houses on this land. But New York City was growing fast, and the water wells in Manhattan were too small and contaminated to meet demand.

So where to import the water from? The Catskills seemed the perfect solution: The region had lots of rain, the altitude was high enough that gravity could help with delivery, and the residents didn't have the political power to oppose such a project. And just as important, the water was "soft," meaning it was low in calcium, the troublesome mineral that clogs up pipes. Its low calcium is also why New York water tastes clean, not metallic. "It's one of the reasons why New York bagels and New York pizza taste so good," says Adam.

So up here in the Catskills, dams were built, fields flooded. The lakes swallowed up eleven towns and thirty-two cemeteries. Gone were farms, blacksmiths, schools, and shops. Thousands of the locals were kicked out and lost their jobs.

"For the people who lived there, it was terrible," says Catskills resident Diane Galusha."There's still a residue of mistrust and bitterness."

A few years ago, during a dry spell, the reservoir receded so much that the remains of Mark's ancestral home were revealed. Mark walked out to the spot and took a photo. He stood in the same stance as an old photo of his grandfather, pipe in hand.

"To be in the actual spot, it was a great feeling. I won't say it's a sacred site, but it's the closest thing to it," he says. "It is really moving. I always remind myself that he worked in the same place I do. They say blood is thicker than water. But in my family, I'm not sure that's true. It's all mixed up in our heritage."

Mark doesn't hold a grudge. His family made out okay. His great-grandfather got a job in construction helping to lay bricks for the reservoir.

But not everyone was so lucky. Hundreds had their lives uprooted. And it's not just the ancestors who paid a price. Even today, Catskills residents still have to conform to super-strict regulations about farming. Their anger shows up on the back of their cars: You can sometimes see bumper stickers around here that read *HELP NEW YORK'S WATER SUPPLY* next to an illustration of a guy peeing into the reservoir.

This is a huge theme I need to remember as part of Project Gratitude: My comfort often comes at the expense of others. I benefit daily from the disruption to this community. I need to be more grateful for these sacrifices.

Adam was hired, in part, to be a peacemaker. He grew up in this area. "I still get heckled once in a while at the grocery store when I'm wearing my DEP shirt," Adam told me. But he says things are on the upswing. He's trying to find solutions that work for both sides (such as pushing for manure storage, which is good for farmers and good for keeping the water free from "organic matter," as it's euphemistically called).

• • •

Next on my Water Appreciation Tour is the tunnel where the water swishes along the bottom, starting its journey south. Adam shows me a filtering screen the size of a pizza pie that holds several curled-up dead trout. And, finally, he takes me to a nearby building where lab-coated scientists poke and prod the water to make sure it's safe.

My guide to the lab, Kirsten Askildsen, is a sneaker-wearing chemist with long brown hair parted in the middle. She's not messing around.

"I have to warn you," she says, before she opens the glass door leading to the labs. "You cannot touch anything in there. Hands to yourself. There is acid that could burn you."

We enter a brightly lit room. There's water in every type of container you can imagine: little flasks, big flasks, beakers, pipes, droppers. I spot a box of tubes filled with water colored in bright Gatorade-like hues.

We walk past a massive freezer with a photo of actor Christopher Walken.

"As in walk-in freezer," Kirsten explains. Scientists do love their puns.

I notice a rack of long glass tubes. They sort of look like a collection of bongs in the dorm room of a dedicated Phish fan.

"We use these to get water samples," Kirsten says.

Every day, teams of DEP workers wade into the reservoirs in thigh-high rubber boots and fill the pipes with samples—a lot of samples. New York water is tested 2.2 million times a year.

They're testing our water for more than two hundred substances. The list is extensive and a little alarming: *E. coli* bacteria, arsenic, silver, and, of course, lead. New York has been lucky and vigilant—our lead content is historically minuscule, unlike, say, Flint, Michigan, which is still suffering from a lead poisoning crisis.

New York has, however, had other problems. After Hurricane Sandy, the water was so muddy, it looked like Yoo-hoo chocolate drink.

To keep our water safe from microorganisms, Kirsten and her colleagues use several weapons, including ultraviolet rays and chlorine. Yes, my hippie aunt may consider this a government conspiracy, but I'm with the CDC, which said the addition of chlorine to drinking water is one of the ten great health achievements of the twentieth century.

"I love New York water," Kirsten says. "I went to Philadelphia, and I couldn't drink the water there. It tasted like cucumber to me."

I could easily stay for weeks and thank a thousand people for my daily water: the valve-makers, the water scientists trying to minimize the effects of climate change, the folks who mow the grass on top of the reservoir dams. "That's a tough job," says Adam. "These guys are stung by bees. They get smashed in the face by a sumac tree. Inevitably, they'll step on a hornet's nest and get stung."

I'll try to thank them soon. Now I have to go home, so I thank Kirsten again and drive south.

● ● ●

When I get back to my apartment, I kiss the boys good night and spritz Sheldon, our tortoise, with some Catskills-born water. Later that night, I take a shower—hot, of course. I send out a mental thanks to the water quality inspectors who wade in thigh boots into the reservoir on chilly February days. They freeze so I can stay comfy.

I climb into bed. I recently told a friend about Project Gratitude, and she said she uses a gratitude trick to fall asleep. As her head rests on her pillow, she'll go through the alphabet from A to Z and try to think of something to be grateful for that starts with each letter—A for her husband Andrew's blueberry pancakes; B for bocce, her favorite game in the summer; etc.

I figure I should give it a try, but maybe focus exclusively on coffee.

A is for Arabica, the tastier variety of coffee bean sold at places like Joe Coffee and Starbucks. I'm grateful to the horti- culturists who developed it.

B is for bags. Thank you to the people in Colombia who make the burlap bags that carry my coffee north.

C is for the customs people. Thank you for letting my coffee through while trying to stop even more addictive drugs.

D is for dockworkers. Thank you for unloading thousands of pounds of coffee every week.

I have my Z at the ready (I've seen Ziploc plastic containers in the Joe Coffee storage bin), but I never get there. I drift off around M or N.

THANKS A THOUSAND...

ED KAUFMANN
*Head of Buying
at Joe Coffee*

CHUNG LEE
Barista

DOUG FLEMING
Inventor of Viora Lid

JAY SORENSEN
Creator of Java Jacket

MARKE JOHNSON
Designer of Joe Coffee Logo

AMARIS GUTIERREZ-RAY
Assistant QC Manager

ROBERTA DUARTE
Production Roaster

LEE HARRISON
Director of Roasting

ERIC HEREDIA
Production Assistant

VLAD KANEVSKY
Production Assistant

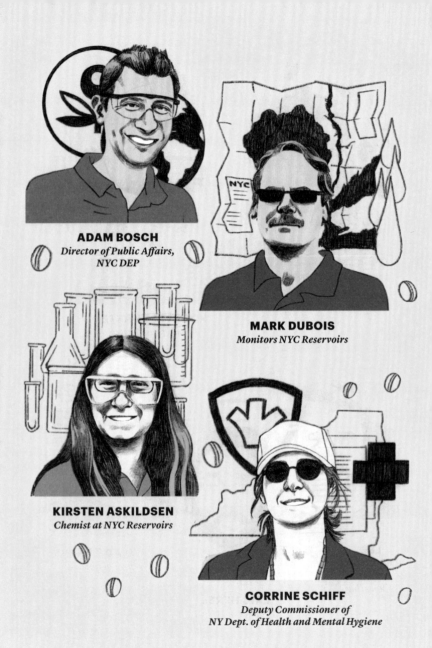

ADAM BOSCH
*Director of Public Affairs,
NYC DEP*

MARK DUBOIS
Monitors NYC Reservoirs

KIRSTEN ASKILDSEN
Chemist at NYC Reservoirs

CORRINE SCHIFF
*Deputy Commissioner of
NY Dept. of Health and Mental Hygiene*

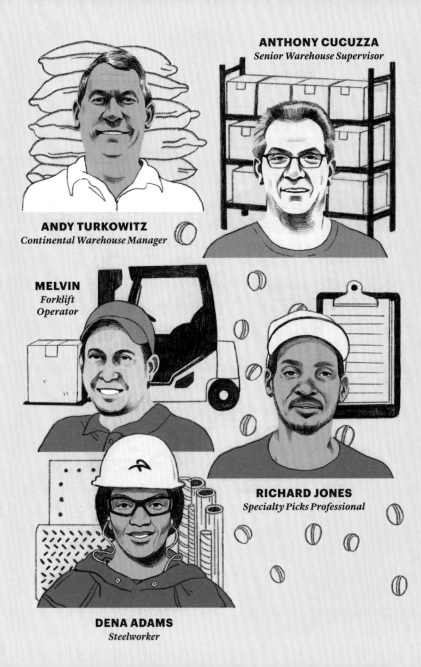

ANDY TURKOWITZ
Continental Warehouse Manager

ANTHONY CUCUZZA
Senior Warehouse Supervisor

MELVIN
Forklift Operator

RICHARD JONES
Specialty Picks Professional

DENA ADAMS
Steelworker

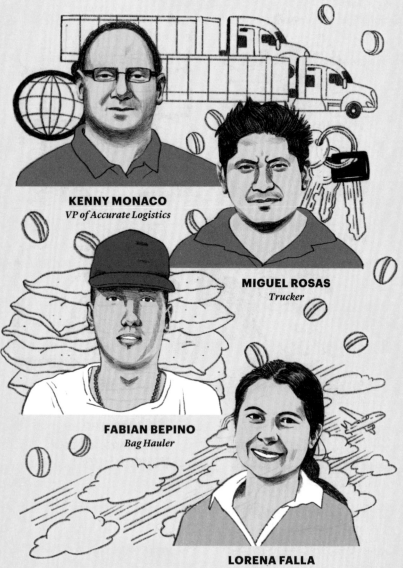

KENNY MONACO
VP of Accurate Logistics

MIGUEL ROSAS
Trucker

FABIAN BEPINO
Bag Hauler

LORENA FALLA
Importer

Coffee Farmers

WILSON GUARNIZO

WILMAR GUARNIZO

YIMMI GUARNIZO

ALEXIS GUARNIZO

5 The Safety Patrol
Thanks for Keeping Me from Dying

This morning, I spend two minutes reading out loud a list of horrible diseases I've found on the Internet.

"I'm pretty sure I don't have Dengue fever," I say to Julie.

"Good to hear."

"Also, I don't have river blindness."

"Happy for you."

This list is part of a gratitude strategy I've been testing out.

A couple of days ago, my ankle started aching and I've been walking with a slight limp. I don't know what caused it. I'm getting to the age where my body parts will break down from what manufacturers call "general wear and tear." I've also noticed my body is louder than ever, with clicks and pops emanating from various joints. When I get up from a chair, my body sounds like it's speaking a dialect of !Kung.

But instead of succumbing to my default complaint mode, I'm trying to put my minor ailments into perspective. Which is why I'm reading this list of diseases that I do *not* have. Admittedly, this is a risky strategy, depending on your mind-set. If you're prone to hypochondria, you might start to think, well, maybe I do have rubella.

For me, though, it's having the desired effect. It reminds me how lucky I am to have relatively good health, at least for now. In the coming years, odds are I'll battle some horrible ailments, but while I'm moderately healthy, I need to be more aware of it. I need to cherish it.

It's a challenge. It's much easier to be grateful for a good thing (a raise at work, a delicious meal) than for the lack of a bad thing. But both are important.

This was reinforced the other day when I checked in with my friend Will MacAskill. Will is an ethics philosopher at Oxford whom I've interviewed for several articles. I find he can give perspective on pretty much any topic.

"What are you grateful for?" I asked him.

"Sometimes I'm just thankful I have arms."

Will's answer is odd, but I like it. These limbs sticking out from my torso are indeed something to be thankful for. They're pretty useful. I'm using them to type this sentence right now.

"It's important to try to be grateful for things that wouldn't even occur to you," Will advised. It's hard not to take the existence of arms for granted. But it's worth the effort.

If you take this line of thinking to its logical endpoint, you wind up being grateful that you exist at all. Again, not an easy task, especially when you don't have time to spend a weekend shrooming in Joshua Tree. But one strategy I've found useful is the memento mori, the reminder of death.

I've been a fan of memento mori ever since I read about their fascinating history. In Roman times, when a general was given a triumphal parade, a slave stood in the chariot with him, whispering in his ear that he was mortal. Death reminders were popular in the Renaissance as well. Many classical paintings have skulls or timepieces in the background to remind viewers of the fleetingness of their earthly existence.

I was inspired by the skulls in old paintings, but didn't like the idea of staring at a macabre cranial bone all day. So a couple of years ago, I found a JPEG of a bright, festive psychedelic skull, and I keep it in a corner of my computer screen.

When it works, it reminds me to savor life, to stress less, to forgive more easily. I hate the phrase YOLO, since it can be an easy excuse to act like an idiot and, say, whack mailboxes with a baseball bat. But I do believe in WOLO: *we* only live once. Live life to its fullest as long as you allow other people to do the same and don't interfere with the U.S. mail.

Okay, back to coffee—which is, in fact, relevant to my thoughts on health and death, because coffee, unlike most of my favorite foods and drinks, isn't so bad for you. According to some studies, it's actually kind of healthy—a fact that I'm profoundly grateful for.

You can find research that shows that coffee lowers the odds of several types of cancer (bladder, breast, prostate, and liver) as well as Alzheimer's. I even found a dubious-sounding study showing that moderate coffee consumption decreases the rate of suicide.

Of course, you can also find downsides to coffee. More than two cups a day can cause sleeplessness and raise cholesterol. There are some still inconclusive studies suggesting a chemical

THANKS A THOUSAND   67

in coffee might be a carcinogen, which an overzealous judge
in California thought required a warning. But I'm going to
embrace my confirmation bias and stick to believing that coffee
is healthy overall.

I should clarify, though. When I say coffee is healthy, I'm
speaking of modern coffee. The coffee in centuries gone by—
along with much of what passed for food and drink—was often
contaminated, dangerous, and just plain revolting.

There are many historical reasons coffee has improved,
but I'd like to single out for special gratitude a nineteenth-
century British scientist named Arthur Hill Hassall. To quote
the book *Terrors of the Table*, a wonderful and horrifying
study of culinary history, Hassall was a "resolute crusader
who eventually turned the tide" and made the world safer for
stomachs.

Hassall began his career as an anatomist, a virtuoso with
the microscope. For years, Hassall and his scientific colleagues
had been hearing reports of impure foods. There were frequent
outbreaks of children dying after eating rotten meat or
produce. So Hassall trained his microscope on Britain's meals.
He became a culinary CSI—starting with what he suspected
was one of the worst offenders: coffee. He secretly bought
coffee at thirty-four different shops in London and put it under
his lens. It was not a pretty sight.

All but two of the thirty-four coffees had impurities. Several
were almost entirely impurities with just a dash of real coffee.
Coffee beans, after all, were expensive. Shopkeepers could jack
up their profits by mixing in cheaper fillers.

And what were those fillers? Well, pour yourself a cup of relatively safe coffee and settle in. Below is just a partial list of impurities found in history's coffees, according to the book *Uncommon Grounds*:

> Almonds, asparagus seeds, baked horse liver, barley, beetroot, bran, bread crusts, brewery waste, brick dust, burnt rags, carrot, chickpeas, chicory, chrysanthemum seeds, coal ashes, cocoa shells, cranberries, currants, dandelion roots, date seeds, dirt, dog biscuits, elderberries, figs, gherkins, horse chestnuts, Jerusalem artichokes, kola nuts, lentils, malt, monkey nuts, mulberries . . .

The list continues to Z, but you get the idea. Incidentally, in case you were wondering, "monkey nuts" are a South American species of shrub, though I'm sure if the price were right, coffee merchants would have happily sprinkled in private parts of simians.

Fraudulent coffees could be dangerous. Around the same time Hassall was inspecting coffee grounds in England, a scandal broke out in New York City. An investigation found that merchants had been dyeing low-quality coffee beans to make them look darker. What was the dye made of? Arsenic and lead. As the *New York Times* wrote in a headline: "Poison in Every Cup of Coffee."

In 1850, Hassall put out a report called "On the Adulteration of Coffee." It caused a hullaballoo. And thanks to his work—and other crusaders who found impurities in all types of other food—the British Parliament eventually acted. It passed the Sale of Food and Drugs Act in 1875. The American government followed suit and formed the department that would later become the FDA.

I'm reminded once again how grateful I am to have been born in 1968, not 1868, because the good old days were not good at all. I firmly believe most nostalgia for the glorious past is delusional thinking. I used to write a magazine column in which, each month, I would research just how horrible the previous centuries were— disease-ridden, dangerous, cruel, racist, sexist, smelly, superstitious, and poisonous. I wrote about food, but also childrearing (opium lozenges to calm kids), clothes (tiny-waisted corsets that deformed women's bodies), and jobs (nightmen, the eighteenth-century workers who would haul manure from houses).

We have huge challenges now, no doubt, but the solution doesn't lie in a return to yesteryear. Sometimes, when I'm feeling particularly annoyed about something—the rattle of the air conditioner, say—I'll repeat a three-word phrase: "Surgery without anesthesia." It's a helpful little mantra: Surgery without anesthesia. When I initially read first-person accounts of eighteenth-century surgery, I was haunted for days, but it sure shut up my whining.

•   •   •

So it's clear: I need to give big thanks to the people who continue the crusade to keep dog biscuits and coal ashes out of my favorite beverages.

Several agencies ensure the safety of what goes in my mouth—the FDA, the U.S. Customs department—but I figure I'll start locally with the New York Department of Health and Mental Hygiene. I set up a call with Corinne Schiff, the deputy commissioner.

"I want to thank you for keeping my food safe," I say when she picks up the phone.

"Well, that's fine," she replies.

Corinne helps manage an army of inspectors who monitor all 24,000 of the city's restaurants. Each restaurant gets a grade—A, B, or C—on how hygienic it is. There is no F grade, because if a restaurant repeatedly fails, it will be shut down. The city closed about five hundred restaurants last year.

My local Joe Coffee is a teacher's pet: It has a big blue A certificate in the front window.

I ask Corinne whether being one of New York's top food safety experts makes it awkward to eat at friends' homes.

"I've been to several dinner parties where people ask me if I'm going to grade their kitchen," Corinne says.

"And do you?"

"No. I don't give grades to homes."

Corinne confesses her own kitchen might not pass the city's inspection. For one thing, at a restaurant, workers aren't supposed to wash their hands in the kitchen sink. Still, Corinne says her kitchen hygiene habits are probably above average for a home. She took a class in food safety, and some lessons stuck.

"I'm a good hand washer," she says. "I try to wash under the fingernails. And I'm a good washer of my fruit. I always wash the outside of the melon."

Every day, the New York inspectors search for restaurants with a high risk of bacteria or rodents. On the Health Department website, you can find a long list of rules. If you break enough of them, your grade drops.

Cutting boards, for instance, should not have nicks or grooves, because that's where bacteria can hide. Cloths for wiping tables must be frequently rinsed in a sanitizing solution. Hot foods need to be kept at 140°F or above.

Some inspectors say they have to hustle right to the kitchen when they arrive—no small talk—to make sure the restaurant staff doesn't have time to cover their sins.

Corinne says that the system is working. Over the last ten years, inspections have increased 70 percent, and food-borne illnesses have dropped precipitously. Salmonella cases from restaurants, for instance, were cut in half.

"I notice that the grading system isn't always beloved," I say. "Some people in the restaurant industry aren't fans."

There's an uncomfortable pause.

"Like, that *New York Post* article," I continue. A few years ago, the *New York Post* ran an op-ed blasting the Health Department as an example of the overreaching nanny state. As the headline blared, we are living under the "Ministry of Mouse-Dropping Enforcement's rotten inspection system."

These inspections, the *Post* complained, were the result of greedy bureaucrats—"health Nazis," as the writer called them—who just want their $45 million in annual fines. The rules were "inimical to first-class cuisine."

The *Post* found a batch of high-profile disgruntled chefs and restaurateurs to comment. Danny Meyer, for instance, told his Twitter followers to "ignore the 'B' letter grade" at a sushi restaurant. He explained that it just meant the sushi chefs refuse to wear rubber gloves. It interferes with their art, and the latex might spoil the subtle flavor of the raw fish.

When I mention the *Post*, Corinne doesn't respond for a few seconds. I can feel the tone of the conversation get colder. Corinne doesn't want to tussle with anti-inspection zealots. She doesn't answer directly, simply replying that the department's goal is that every restaurant get an A grade.

After we hang up, I email the Health Department to ask if I can come along on an inspection and thank the inspector in person.

"We are unable to grant that request," the press officer writes back.

Ugh. I feel my face getting hot. I start typing a condescending email to her explaining that this is exactly why people hate the government. Her secrecy is stupid and counterproductive. "You should take a lesson from the EPA, which gave me a tour of reservoirs."

Before I send the email, I catch myself. Is that a good use of my anger? Clearly, I've got a ways to go before achieving gratitude nirvana. I'm still irritated more than 50 percent of the time. I shouldn't let one little rejection throw me into a rage.

I delete my email, but I do think the press officer made a mistake. Unlike the *Post*, I'm not opposed to the Ministry of Mouse-Dropping Enforcement. I'm grateful for it. I think the government should do a bit of nannying, as long as the nannying is rational and doesn't overreach.

• • •

My thoughts on this crystallized a few days ago when my friend sent me an essay called "I, Pencil," which was written in 1957 by a libertarian scholar named Leonard E. Read.

When I started to read the essay, I was alarmed by how similar it was to my coffee project—minus the gratitude and caffeine. Written in the first person from the point of view of the pencil, the essay details the work of the many people and raw materials that go into making a pencil. The cedar trees for the wood. The rubber for the eraser. "Think of all the thousands and thousands of skills . . . the mining of ore, the making of steel and its refinement into saws, axes, motors; the logging camps with their beds and mess halls."

My first reaction was, "Hey! This author somehow retroactively ripped off my idea."

And it is true in some ways—our projects are very similar. But it soon became clear to me that, in other ways, our insights diverge sharply.

The main thesis of "I, Pencil" is that there should be little to no government interference in the smooth workings of the capitalist machine. It's an ode to the free market. The foreword is by none other than laissez-faire superhero Milton Friedman. Friedman writes: "Economies can hardly be 'planned' when not one soul possesses all the know-how and skills to produce a simple pencil. . . . If you can become aware of the miraculousness which a pencil symbolizes, you can help save the freedom mankind is so unhappily losing."

So "I, Pencil" argues that by tracing a product's diverse origins, you'll understand why the government should butt out. Yet I had the opposite reaction. I found that tracing the origins of a pencil or cup of coffee shows that we need smart, visionary politicians to help us.

I'm a believer in capitalism—I think it's the best way we've found so far to structure a society. But I don't buy the laissez-faire idea. I think we need regulations. I'm in favor of a superego to control the market's id. I'm in favor of long-range thinking to balance stockholders' lust for immediate profits. I think we need infrastructure to help us get the pencil and coffee safely into our hands. And I think we also need high-level coordination to keep us from playing with lead-paint-coated toys, eating salmonella steaks, and baking ourselves into oblivion with overreliance on fossil fuels.

Don't get me wrong. I think there's huge room for improvement in government. I'm certainly no fan of the current administration. And a lot of current regulation is arcane, outdated, and irrational—including, perhaps, some restaurant regulations.

But we do need government, so I give thanks to the American government and the peaceful transfer of power. It's amazing, and I never acknowledge that. So thank you for existing, you flawed but noble three-branched institution!

6 The Movers
Thanks for Lugging My Coffee Around the World

The walk from my apartment to Joe Coffee takes under four minutes. I go two blocks, just past the deli and a barbershop.

The coffee's trip to Joe Coffee is a little more arduous.

"It still blows my mind to think of the distance a coffee bean has to travel to get to your cup," Ed recently said.

By the time I take a sip, the bean has been on a nine-month-long journey of 2,500 miles across the equator. It has traveled by motorcycles, trucks, boats, vans, pallets, shoulders, and forklifts. It's been stored in buckets, bags, tubs, and metal containers the size of a small apartment. It's come down a tree, descended a mountain, docked in ports, navigated customs, been loaded into a warehouse, rattled around on flatbeds.

It's like a tiny caffeinated *Amazing Race* contestant.

It won't be easy, but I need to thank the many, many people who carry my coffee bean to me.

I start with the truckers. I drive a rental car to New Jersey, passing the Thomas Edison Rest Stop (which reminds me to thank Edison for light bulbs at Joe Coffee, even if he was a bit of a weasel who screwed fellow inventor Nikola Tesla), and pull into an enormous parking lot in the town of Clifton.

This is the home of Accurate Logistics, which has a fleet of several dozen eighteen-wheelers, most of them out on the road right now. The trucks carry Joe Coffee from the port to the warehouse in Jersey. In the parking lot, I'm met by Kenny Monaco, Accurate's vice president and a New Jersey native.

"Thank you," I tell Kenny. "I just want to acknowledge that I wouldn't have my cup of coffee every morning without you."

"It's funny you should say that," Kenny says, "because I've seen people go into big box stores, and ask, 'Do you have any microwaves?' And the guy at the store will say, 'Yeah, we got some in the back.' Well, those microwaves didn't just magically appear in the back. Somebody put them there. And we're the ones who did it. It's good to be acknowledged."

Kenny doesn't haul a lot of microwaves. His company specializes in coffee and floor tiles. But his point is well taken.

For most of my life, not counting a brief obsession with Tonka toys at age seven, I thought of trucks as an annoyance. They're loud and flatulent. They wake me up in the morning. When I'm driving on the highway, trucks either make me aggravated (why am I stuck behind this hunk of metal creeping up the hill?) or anxious (when is this truck going to drift into my lane and run me into a ditch?).

But on my drive to New Jersey today, I tried to switch my point of view. If I'm going to enjoy my coffee—or my strawberries or my spiral notebooks or my backgammon set—I need to stop being so petty. I can't have it both ways. I need to be thankful for trucks and truck drivers—at least until Amazon drones take over.

I tell Kenny that I'm trying to reform my perspective.

He nods. "You know that bumper sticker, 'America Stops Without Trucks,'" he says. "It's true."

•   •   •

I leave the truck depot and drive for half an hour to an enormous beige rectangular building—the Continental Terminals coffee warehouse.

"Thank you for my coffee. And thank you for meeting me," I say to the warehouse manager, Andy Turkowitz, as I greet him in the front office.

"You want to go inside?" he asks.

Andy opens a steel door and I step through it. Here's what I say next, according to my audio recorder: "Holy shit! This is insane!"

What I'm reacting to is the sheer quantity of coffee in my sightline. Picture a burlap sack with 150 pounds of coffee beans. Now picture a tower of burlap sacks piled fifteen feet high. Then imagine hundreds of these coffee towers, stretching back four football fields. The labels on the sacks identify coffee from Ecuador, New Zealand, Ethiopia . . . all over.

I later did some calculations: The warehouse contains 470,000 sacks of coffee, each with about 150 pounds of beans. If you brew every bean in this warehouse, you'd have 3 billion cups of coffee. That's enough to supply the entire New York police department for three hundred years.

This warehouse is one of the key stops on my coffee beans' trip to my cup. The beans travel by ship from Colombia, arrive at a Jersey port, and are driven to this warehouse, where they relax for several months before being trucked to the Brooklyn roastery.

"Come this way," Andy says, leading me down an aisle in between the stacks. A beeping forklift bears down on us, and we duck behind a pile of bags. "You don't want to get hit before you can write your book," Andy says.

The warehouse is loud and not just because of the beeping forklifts. There are fans with blades the size of surfboards and rumbling trucks backing into bays.

And the aroma—it's overwhelming. I started to smell the coffee in my car with the windows closed from several blocks away. "You're lucky you're not doing a book on chocolate," Andy tells me. "The smell at the cocoa warehouse will make your eyes water."

The coffee warehouse has about thirty-five workers, mostly men: Some are lugging the bags onto pallets. Some are sweeping mounds of spilled coffee beans off the floor. Some are wrapping the loads of coffee in clear plastic. Some are weighing the bags on a scale the size of my kitchen.

What they aren't doing is sipping coffee. Andy apologizes that he can't offer me a cup; their coffee maker is at another warehouse while they remodel the offices here. Coffee, coffee all around and not a drop to drink.

Andy has brown hair and a short-sleeve white shirt. He was born in Brooklyn, the son of a pharmacist. His grandfather was close friends with gangster Meyer Lansky. I decide not to press for details. One of Andy's first jobs was emptying quarters from coin-operated candy machines.

He likes to bust chops. "What year'd you start working here?" he asks a gray-haired guy who works with forklift operators. "When was it? 1850?"

He reminds me of a slimmer, modern-day Ralph Kramden. If I had to choose one adjective for him, I'd say he's beleaguered. He almost seems to relish it.

He's beleaguered by botched orders. "You get that extra order I sent?" he asks one of his deputies over his cell phone, as we walk. "That's got to go out, dude, because [name withheld] fucked me."

He's beleaguered by sloppy work. "See these bags? They aren't stacked properly." He points to a pile of bags that do look dangerously close to collapsing, like a giant Jenga puzzle. He nudges a bag to the left to make the pile more stable.

He's beleaguered by vendors. "I'm in a holy war with the forklift company."

He's beleaguered by the threat of pests. "Moths are a problem. We have this thing that emits pheromones." He shows me a small white box on the wall. "It turns the moths homosexual so they don't breed." (I look it up later. This is actually how it works.)

And he's beleaguered by some of his clients, a small subset of whom give him a big pain in the butt. For instance, the clients for specialty coffee—not the big chains, which are easy, and just want a heap of the same bags. The specialty coffee buyers go through the warehouse with a list. "They pick bags like you would at a grocery store, one at a time. And you can't use hooks to move the bags because they're worried that it'd puncture the bag. You have to move them by hand. Drives me insane."

In fact, Andy believes we might be in a specialty coffee bubble. "I think specialty coffee might be like the pet rock. I mean, how many little stores can there be?"

I ask Andy whether it feels good that the coffee in his warehouse brings joy to millions of people. Andy looks at me, his eyebrows knit. It's as if I just asked him if he enjoys being a Buddhist monk who meditates ten hours a day.

"Well, let me ask you this," I say. "What are you thankful for?"

"My paycheck," he says, laughing.

Okay, so Andy is not the sentimental type.

As Andy and I walk through the aisles, I call out thanks to the other people working in the warehouse. "Thanks for my coffee!" The sweeper nods at me. The guy who wraps the sacks in plastic gives me a thumbs-up. The guy loading the container looks at me with an eyebrow raised.

A forklift operator asks me, "Hey, you want to take over my job for a bit?"

I glance at Andy for approval. He shakes his head. No dice. Insurance issues.

•   •   •

When I get home I turn my attention to pallets. At both the warehouse and the truck depot, I saw dozens of pallets, those wooden platforms about the size of a foosball table. The coffee bags are loaded onto the pallets, and the pallets are in turn loaded onto trucks and boats.

I'd never given pallets much thought, so I decided to do a little research. Turns out they are a huge deal. A couple of years ago *Slate* published an article about pallets with the following headline: "The Single Most Important Object in the Global Economy," which is probably one of the Top Fifty Most Hyperbolic Headlines About Shipping Logistics Ever!

But it's a good article, and the gist is correct: Pallets move everything. If you're reading the paper-and-ink version of this book, it probably took a ride on a pallet. If you're reading the book on a smartphone or a computer, those were also on pallets. The pants or skirt you're wearing, they've been on pallets. The toothpaste and dish soap you used this morning, pallet passengers too.

Tom Vanderbilt, who wrote the *Slate* article, puts it this way: "For an invisible object, [pallets] are everywhere: There are said to be billions circulating through the global supply chain. Some 80 percent of all U.S. commerce is carried on pallets. So widespread is their use that they account for, according to one estimate, more than 46 percent of total U.S. hardwood lumber production."

Pallets save billions of hours of work every year. They're designed to allow forklifts to pick them up and move the merchandise all at once without unloading. And pallets fit snugly next to each other in the truck or warehouse for maximum storage.

Pallets are even considered war heroes. In World War II, the Allies used this new technology to ship food and ammunition around the world. So thank you, pallets, for saving democracy.

I wrote down the name of one of the pallets I spotted at the warehouse. It was made by a small New Jersey–based company called Jimenez Pallets. I dial the number.

"Is Rafael Jimenez there?" I ask.

"Yes, that's me." He has a thick Latino accent.

"Oh, great. I want to thank you."

"For what?"

"I'm a writer, and I'm thanking everyone who helped make my cup of coffee a reality. And your pallets carried my coffee. So thank you."

"No problem," he says.

His tone is flat. I wonder if I'm being helpful or just intrusive.

"Can I ask you something for real? Do you appreciate getting thanked, or is it a waste of your time in the middle of your workday?" I say.

Suddenly Rafael warms up. "You never *ever* waste my time."

"Oh, that's good to hear."

"You are a very wonderful person. I really appreciate you taking the time to reach out and thank me."

He seemed earnestly happy, or else he's as talented at acting as he is at making wooden platforms.

Next I call Parkway Pest Services, which keeps the insects out of the warehouse. A woman answers.

"This may sound strange, but I want to thank you."

There's a long pause. "Okay, I'm going to hear you out."

I explain my project, and end with "So . . . thank you."

"Absolutely," she chuckles. "Glad we could help."

"Yeah, I've never found any bugs or mice in my coffee. So thanks for that."

"I'm really glad you never found any bugs or mice in your coffee. And thank *you*. You made my day. You put a smile on my face."

I hang up. I'm on a high.

I was kind of dreading these phone calls. But I'm actually getting a nice little flush in my cheeks. It's like making an anti-crank phone call. It's the opposite of what I did with my friends in middle school. Not to mention that these phone calls are nudging up my total—I'm up to 526 thank-yous.

On a roll, I decide I should call the lumber company that provides the wood for the pallets. I call Rafael back to ask him where he gets his wood.

"I'm working now. I'll email you later," he says brusquely, and hangs up.

Okay, now I think I am officially wasting his time. He never emails.

The next day I go out to lunch with my friend Brian, and I tell him that I'm busy thanking all the people who helped transport my coffee. "You know, like the dockworkers and the truck drivers," I say.

Brian responds, "Are you going to thank the drug dealers who sell meth to the truck drivers so they can drive all night?"

Dang.

Brian's comment may be flippant, but it sticks in my mind. It's brought up an interesting problem. Not everyone who helps get my coffee to me is a good person. Or at least not everyone is acting in a way that is good for the world. Some are doing great damage and inflicting much suffering: There are probably foremen who harass their workers. There are likely corrupt bureaucrats. There are executives at Exxon who provide the gas for the trucks at Accurate Logistics, but whose quest for annual profits is choking our atmosphere and helping to roast our planet and imperil the lives of any great-grandkids I may have.

So . . . does the CEO of Exxon deserve my thanks? I'm not sure. I decide to email my gratitude expert, the psychologist Scott Barry Kaufman. He responds the same day:

"What a *fascinating* conundrum! I wish my class hadn't ended, or else I'd outsource this to my students. I think the answer to your question is similar to the answer to the question: How can I have compassion and loving-kindness for my enemies? I think you can have gratitude that someone helped you in a particular way, while simultaneously wish for the reduction of suffering of that person. If the CEO of Exxon, for instance, got some of his own insecurities and defenses under control, he'd be less motivated for greed and profit, and more motivated for growth and humanitarianism. Under such a situation, his own suffering would be reduced *and* the world would be a better place. Two in one."

•   •   •

I like Scott's compassionate view of the Exxon CEO's conflicted soul, but I wonder if perhaps he's giving the CEO too much credit for self-reform. I decide I need to try to combine gratitude and activism. So I click on the Exxon website and type an email.

> Dear Mr. Darren Woods, CEO of Exxon,
>
> Thank you for providing the gasoline that fuels the truck that brings my coffee to me. I know you and your employees work very hard.
>
> I love coffee. I hope to drink it for a long time.
>
> I hope that climate change caused by our world's overreliance on fossil fuel doesn't ravage the planet and make it impossible to have coffee farms in the future. I hope we embrace alternative energies more aggressively than we are doing now.
>
> Anyway, to reiterate, thanks for helping me get my coffee! It's delicious.
>
> Best,
> A.J. Jacobs

When I press send, I realize I have just written possibly the most passive-aggressive thank-you note in history. *Thank you, now please change.* I'm still waiting to hear back.

7 The Extractors
Thanks for Getting All the Raw Materials

Exxon's oil, of course, is just one of dozens of raw materials needed to conjure my coffee into existence. You need wood for the paper cup, rubber for truck tires, copper for the wiring in the roasters.

Many of these materials are extracted from the earth by corporations like Exxon, which probably don't have humanity's well-being as their number one priority. Many a shady, short-sighted thing has been done in search of quarterly profits.

But these companies also have thousands of hardworking employees who are just trying to earn an honest living. Those people deserve my thanks, which is why I've traveled to Burns Harbor, Indiana, to visit one of the biggest still-operating steel mills in the United States. In the reception area I don the requisite protective gear—a helmet, a fire-retardant coat, earplugs, and a pair of white gloves.

"Those gloves will be black by the end of the day," says Larry, my assigned guide. "You'll help us clean the handrails around here."

Larry is a tall, gray-haired man with a big laugh, a big stride, and an American flag sticker on his hard hat. He's worked in steel his whole life, as did his dad and grandfather.

As Larry says, steel is everywhere. It's practically womb to tomb. When I was born, I was weighed on a steel scale. When I die, I'll probably be buried in a steel-lined coffin.

And my coffee wouldn't exist without steel. The ships and trains and trucks that carry the beans are made of steel, as are the stop signs and bridges and docks on their routes. Steel is in coffee scoopers and roasting machines, refrigerators and spoons. The owners of this mill—the Luxembourgian/Indian company ArcelorMittal—churn out steel that can be found in almost every vehicle on the road, so it certainly played a role in my morning drink.

Larry's coworker gives us some final words of wisdom before we head off. "Never, ever, ever run in a steel mill. Unless Larry runs. Then run real fast."

We drive along puddle-covered roads that connect the plant's many buildings, and I marvel at the scope of the place. We pass by hills of black coal and a field covered with hundreds of steel coils that resemble giant rolls of duct tape. We enter a huge building with a huge crane lifting a huge bucket the size of my bedroom. The bucket is filled with a glowing orange steel soup that, when tipped over, glides into a furnace.

"That's how we pour the coffee into the mug," Larry says.

I won't go into all the technical details (mostly because I didn't understand them), but the basic recipe for the steel is: take iron pellets shipped from Minnesota, mix with limestone, sinter, and coke (a form of charcoal), and heat to over four thousand degrees.

The steel gets so hot, you need special brick to hold it—brick, incidentally, that is imported from China. As the steel is cooled, it's molded and sliced into sheets or ribbons and sent off to carmakers and dishwasher factories.

For the next six hours, I experience sensory overload. I see showers of sparks and geysers of water. I hear the clanking and creaking as a series of glowing rectangles of steel—each as big as a king mattress—bump down the conveyer belt. I see men tending the furnace dressed in what look like white space suits from a 1950s sci-fi film. I meet a woman whose entire job, eight hours a day, is to stare at a scrolling sheet of steel as it passes by, looking for imperfections and pockmarks in the metal river.

At lunchtime Larry takes me to a conference room with a sandwich tray on the table. I'd asked if I could personally thank some of the steelworkers, and three of them have agreed to meet me. There's Joe Sirokie, a stout maintenance guy who has been at the plant for forty-two years; Pat Fisher, an electrician with a gray beard and plaid shirt who started forty-three years ago; and Shannon Duncan, a crane operator.

"How long have you worked here, Shannon?" I ask.

"I've been here twenty years," she says.

"Punk!" says Pat, laughing.

"Yeah, I'm still green," Shannon says.

Shannon has shoulder-length brown hair and wears jeans and tan work boots. A former dental assistant, she lives with her husband and four German shepherds.

I ask Shannon about her job. She spends her days sitting in the cab of a crane attached to a wall. To lift the sixty thousand-pound coils, Shannon operates three control boxes—two for the crane and one to raise and lower the hook.

"It's a lot about multitasking," she says.

Depending on the day, Shannon says, work at the mill ranges from freezing to sweltering. It can get hot enough to cook dinner, which is not meant as a metaphor.

"One year, for Thanksgiving, we cooked a turkey in a steel coil," Shannon said. "It came out cherry red. It was actually pretty good."

Which is surprising, as there's often the smell of sulfur at the plant, an odor that soaks into the steelworkers' hair and clothes, and oozes out of their pores when they sweat. "It takes a couple of days to get it out," says Pat. "Ask my wife. Or Shannon's dogs."

Another gas in the mill, carbon monoxide, is odorless but far more worrisome. All the steelworkers wear a carbon monoxide monitor on the shoulder of their shirts. It looks like a small walkie-talkie. Both Shannon and Joe say they've gotten carbon monoxide poisoning that laid them up for a couple of days.

"It's the worst case of flu that you would ever want to get," says Shannon.

"The headache was just pounding," says Joe. "Like the worst hangover."

The threat of carbon monoxide is always on their minds.

"Every morning," Pat says, "you have to pay attention to

where the wind is blowing, so you know where to go if there's a leak."

I notice that the two PR people in the room have smiles that are looking increasingly strained. Almost like they've gotten a whiff of sulfur themselves.

Later, the PR folks will stress to me that they take every precaution that they can. It's a fair point. Steel is much less dangerous than it used to be decades ago, when mangled body parts and fatal injuries were common (Larry's grandfather died from getting caught in some steel machinery). Injuries at the plant have declined 94 percent in the last thirty years.

Better training and omnipresent signs have probably helped. Everywhere you look you see warnings: HIGH VOLTAGE. TIPOVER HAZARD. STOP, LOOK AND LISTEN. TAKE 2, THINK IT THROUGH. There's even a crumpled red van left by the railroad tracks as a cautionary reminder; the van was totaled by an oncoming train.

I ask Shannon, Joe, and Pat what they like best about their job.

"I'm not sorry I stayed here," says Joe, who had considered leaving to work in the aircraft industry. "It paid for two kids to go through college, and a house and a car and everything else."

Shannon talks about the camaraderie. "Nothing is better than working with my team."

And they take pride in their labor. Whenever they see a beam on a bridge, they search for the label to see if it's one of theirs. "My mother-in-law's house in Florida has Bethlehem steel siding on it," says Shannon. (Bethlehem was the former name of the plant, until it was taken over by ArcelorMittal.) "She had one of the old Bethlehem boxes in the garage, and I said, 'Don't get rid of the box. I want it.'"

As lunch ended, I thank them for their part in making my coffee a reality.

"You're welcome," Joe says. He invites me to stay and talk more, but the PR people don't think that's a great idea. Time for me to leave before there's more conversation about gas leaks.

"We're here anytime you want to come back," Joe says. "Shannon will cook a turkey for you."

●   ●   ●

When I return to New York I take stock. I'm getting closer to a thousand. I feel like I've spread some goodwill. But I'm still worried about my gratitude devolving into complacency.

"I want to figure out if there's a way to make my gratitude useful to the people on the chain," I say to Julie.

"If you really want to feel like you're making a difference," Julie says, "you could give up coffee for a year and donate the money you save to charity."

Abstaining from coffee for a year? It's a solid idea. It also fills me with dread. Should I abandon my beloved daily beverage ritual? I call up Oxford philosopher Will MacAskill again to see if that's the properly moral thing to do.

"You could make a good argument that you should *not* give up coffee," says Will.

"Thank God," I say.

"The argument is this: Your typical American probably isn't going to uproot and move to the developing world and become a saint. Knowing that, how can you ensure you do the most good? One way is to splurge on stuff that is not too expensive but that gives you great pleasure. You don't really spend much of your income on coffee. So you can splurge on that. But on bigger items, like cars and apartments, you should spend less and donate the balance to charity."

"I like that," I say. "The idea is to be penny-foolish and pound-wise."

"Right."

So I can rationalize drinking coffee, as long as I make an effort to cut back on big-ticket items—we don't need a car in New York, nor do I need fancy clothes. I promise Will that, though I'll keep drinking coffee, I'll try to be more generous.

"Maybe I should donate to charities related to coffee," I tell him, "like a farmer commune in South America? Or a water charity?"

Will pauses. He has given more thought to the ethics of donating money than perhaps anyone on earth. He's a founder of the Effective Altruism Movement. The idea of Effective Altruism is to rigorously calculate which charities help the most lives on a per-dollar basis. It's moneyball for saving the world. Compassion meets number-crunching.

In Will's opinion, I shouldn't give to a charity because it overlaps with my coffee project, just as I shouldn't give to music schools for underprivileged children just because I love Beethoven. Instead I should look for the charity that does the most good for the most people. Mosquito nets are highly effective, as are de-worming campaigns in Africa.

With that caveat, Will says that several water charities are doing good work, including one called Dispensers for Safe Water. Later that week, I make a donation equal to the amount I spend on coffee every year.

Will's rigorous ethics have inspired me to make another change. Instead of using a new paper coffee cup every day, I've started to bring my steel water flask to coffee shops. Yes, I know. Call Oslo and alert the Nobel Prize committee! But it makes me feel slightly less powerless, and since climate change threatens coffee farms, it's in my best long-term interest.

Today, I stopped at a café downtown on my way to a meeting, flask in hand.

"I'd like a small cup, please," I said to the barista.

"Sure," he said.

"Oh, and would you mind using this?" I held up my water flask.

"No problem."

The barista had already started filling up a paper cup, so he poured the coffee from the paper cup into my flask and tossed the paper cup in the garbage. Great. A total waste.

Lesson learned: Don't dilly-dally when it comes to climate change.

8 The Farmers
Thanks for Growing My Coffee

It's been five months and roughly seven hundred thank-yous. It's finally time for my big pilgrimage to the source, the home of the coffee trees. My trip down to Colombia consists of increasingly rustic modes of transportation.

I start by taking a jet down to Bogotá, where the airport has multiple images of the mythical Juan Valdez. In the Bogotá airport hotel, I meet Ed, who has been bouncing around South America for more than a week. He's tired and fighting a cold, but chipper. He's wearing what he calls his "Indiana Jones" hat and carrying a bag with his on-the-road kit: coffee beans and an air press. He makes me a cup in the hotel lobby. The beans are Ethiopian, which seems almost treasonous. Ed explains he still loves Colombian coffee; it's just that he wants some variety— and he doesn't want to risk not having his fix.

"Even though we're visiting a coffee farm, we can't be guaranteed we'll drink coffee there," Ed says. "I've been on farms surrounded by coffee beans, and had to battle a lack-of-caffeine headache."

Next, Ed and I board a cozy, knees-to-the-chin propeller plane and land in a small city called Neiva. We climb into a van for a four-hour ride to an even smaller town called Pitalito. It's a town, Ed tells me, that is known for two stimulant crops. Coffee is the legal one.

After which we get in the back of a pickup truck for a ninety-minute drive up a mountain to the coffee farm. We're joined by a woman named Lorena, who lives in Colombia and works for the import company.

It's a beautiful ride . . . and highly uncomfortable. We jounce along the rock-strewn road, occasionally letting out involuntary "*oofs*." We grab the side of the truck as it hugs tight curves overlooking cliffs. I spot the driver doing something with his right hand that I really wish I hadn't seen: the sign of the cross.

I take some deep breaths to calm down. It smells a bit like burning tires. Over the next few minutes, the aroma slowly becomes more agricultural.

"You can smell the coffee," Ed says. "And you can smell the poop. You know, when we're in New York, we have all this fancy equipment. We have our moisture testers and digital scales. But it all really comes down to dirt and mud and rain and cow shit."

At a red light in a small town, we see a man in a purple T-shirt hoping to get some spare change—he's balancing on a unicycle while juggling machetes. As we wait for the light to turn green, he drops his machetes twice. I hand him some pesos from my backpack, figuring it might help pay for potential finger reattachment surgery.

We pass blue and pink brick houses with women on the porches sweeping the dust away. Our truck idles as a herd of cattle crosses the road, their neck wattles bouncing as they walk by. We see barbed wire and cemeteries and hawks circling above.

Ed has given me some background. This farm is a small one, owned by the Guarnizo family, which has nine brothers and one sister. The only visitors in the last year have been us and one other buyer. Ed's been working with the Guarnizos for five years. He says he pays well above fair trade price—and he's even prouder that he uses contracts that span multiple years, so that if there's a bad crop, the family still gets the same amount of money. He could probably find cheaper beans at bigger farms that would be just as good, but he likes supporting the small farms.

"Now, I should tell you, the Guarnizo brothers are not overly emotive," he says. "You can see it in the photos of my visits. The first time, none of them were smiling. They were like, 'We'll see if this guy pays us.' The second year, more smiles. Third year, even more smiles. So I think they're warming up to me." But, he says, there are limits. "I once tried to give them a hug, and I got kind of a side hug."

We make a hard left into a steep driveway arched by trees. I duck several times but the branches still manage to thwack me in the forehead.

We are here. The Guarnizo farm. We're in front of the main house, which is painted light yellow and has a corrugated metal roof. Several enormous chickens—the size of full-grown pit bulls—strut and cluck. There's a blue satellite dish on the porch, and inside there's a child watching *Madagascar: Escape 2*.

The landscape is drop-dead gorgeous. Fog-shrouded peaks in the distance, miles of dark, lush green.

As we hop out of the back of the pickup, the brothers come to meet us. There are six of them wearing jeans, boots, and soccer jerseys in a variety of colors. A couple of the brothers and the sister are off on a trip.

Ed is right, they aren't overly emotive. Unlike when I met Chung, the extroverted barista, there will not be a lot of hugging today. They give us quiet "*holas*" and handshakes.

The oldest brother, Wilmar, who is squat and broad-shouldered, seems to be the one in charge. "Do you want to see the coffee trees?" he asks, in Spanish.

We walk a hundred yards to a patch of trees. The trees are shorter than I expected, about the same height as I am. I wouldn't have known they were coffee trees; there are no beans visible. Instead, the trees are filled with little red or yellow fruits that look like grape tomatoes. The coffee cherries, they're called. Hidden in each cherry is the bean that produces my morning drink.

Wilmar straps a yellow bucket around my shoulders and tells me I should experience picking the beans.

As the Guarnizos watch, I pluck a cherry off the tree and drop it in my bucket. The fruit gives a little resistance as I twist and tug it off the branch, but not much. I pluck another and another. I'm getting into the rhythm. The bottom of my pail is now covered with cherries.

I show my haul to Wilmar.

He smiles and shakes his head in gentle disappointment. Lorena, the Colombian woman from the import company, is more blunt. "*¡No! ¡No! ¡No! No contrato para ti,*" she says, laughing. No contract for me. I'm fired.

The cherries I picked are the wrong color. Too green. The good cherries—the ones with the most sugar—are a particular shade of red, about the same color as Twizzlers. Cherries on the same tree ripen at different times, so you have to be selective.

At Wilmar's urging I take a bite of a cherry. It's much sweeter than I expected. Odd that it hides within it such a bitter little nugget.

The brothers have picked thousands, maybe millions of these cherries over their lifetime. They inherited the farm from their dad and have been working on it since they were kids. They do everything—pick the cherries, buy the fertilizer, and hire additional workers during harvest season.

"Where'd your father get the coffee trees?" I ask.

"From his dad," Wilmar says.

"And where'd he get them?"

"From his dad."

I ask Wilmar what it's like to pick cherries all day.

"It's hard," he says in Spanish. "The sun, the rain. But it can also be very calm, very quiet."

"What do you do to pass the time?" I ask.

"We sing songs. You can too if you want."

"You don't want to hear that."

Let me pause here for a moment to state the obvious: I am lucky. That was the thought going through my mind as I took the bucket's strap off my shoulders. I'd just picked coffee beans for ten minutes as research for a book. I didn't pick coffee beans because I had no other job options and needed to earn money to feed my family, which is the situation of thousands of migrant workers. I picked coffee by choice, not necessity.

And how did I arrive at the luxury of having this choice? Well, mostly luck.

I've been obsessed with luck for many years, and especially with the debate over whether our lives are ruled by randomness, or whether we are the powerful captains of our own fates.

It's an ancient debate, of course. When I wrote a book about the Bible, I learned the scriptures contain both points of view. In Proverbs, the reader is told over and over: Work hard, and you'll be rewarded on this earth. If you follow the rules, if you're not lazy, your crops will flourish and your offspring will be plentiful. This line of thinking has persisted. You can see it in Ayn Rand novels and the ideals of the American Dream and the Puritan work ethic.

But there's another way of looking at the world. The very next chapter following Proverbs is Ecclesiastes, the most modern and philosophical of the Bible's books. Ecclesiastes says: "The race is not to the swift, nor the battle to the strong, nor bread to the wise, nor riches to the intelligent, nor favor to the men of skill; but time and chance happen to them all." In other words: Don't be prideful. Fate is fickle. More than fickle—fate has Borderline Personality Disorder.

The real world is no doubt a combination of luck and skill, but I lean strongly toward Ecclesiastes. If I had to put numbers to it, 20 percent of my fate has been determined by hard work and persistence, and 80 percent has been cosmic Powerball.

Luck determined that I was born in the developed world. Luck determined that I was the son of parents who could afford to send me to an expensive college. Luck determined my genetic makeup. And my career? It's been filled with random breaks. At age twenty-three, I was getting ready to give up on writing and apply to psychology grad school when I sent off a Hail Mary letter addressed only to "Agent at ICM." It somehow got out of the slush pile and landed on the desk of an Elvis-loving literary agent. He thought my idea for an Elvis-themed book might work. If he'd been a Springsteen fan instead, I might be teaching psychology at a small college.

I'm not dismissing the need for effort and persistence. Those who worked their way up from the bottom, who didn't have the advantages I had, need effort and persistence even more than I did. I also acknowledge that, to a certain extent, you make your own luck and create your own opportunities. But only to a certain extent. You also need pure luck. As Barack Obama said in a postpresidential interview with David Letterman,

"I worked hard and I've got some talent, but there are a lot of hardworking, talented people out there. There was an element of chance to it, this element of serendipity."

I agree with our former president. There are millions of hardworking, persistent people around the world living below the poverty line. I believe there are thousands of could-have-been Meryl Streeps working as waitresses because they didn't get the lucky breaks. There are thousands of alternative-universe Steve Jobs working on assembly lines in factories.

Here's why I'm a fan of thanking our lucky stars every day: it helps with forgiving yourself your failures; it cuts down on celebrity worship and boosts humility; and, perhaps most important, it makes us more compassionate.

This is how psychologist David DeSteno puts it in his book *Emotional Success.*

> Recent research suggests that being prompted to recognize luck can encourage generosity. For example, Yuezhou Huo, a former research assistant of mine, designed an experiment in which she promised subjects a cash prize in exchange for completing a survey about a positive thing that had recently happened to them. She asked one group of participants to list factors beyond their control that contributed to the event, a second group to list personal qualities and actions that contributed to it, and a control group to simply explain why the good thing had happened. After completing the survey, subjects were given an opportunity to donate some or all of their reward to charity.

Those who had been prompted to credit external causes—many mentioned luck, as well as factors such as supportive spouses, thoughtful teachers, and financial aid—donated 25 percent more than those who'd been asked to credit personal qualities or choices. Donations from the control group fell roughly midway between those from the other two groups.

Acknowledging the role of chance helps pump up compassion. And compassion is a muscle that I need to work on. It doesn't come naturally to me. I need to remember, with a few flaps of the butterfly wings, I could have easily been anyone on this coffee chain instead of the consumer. I need to acknowledge this without devolving into condescension, because I don't want to assume that I'm happier than the people working on a coffee farm. Perhaps living among the beautiful fog-draped mountains and harvesting the land is a more fulfilling life than what I have. What I am saying is that I'm lucky enough to have more options. I can choose to visit and spend a day picking coffee beans.

It's a weird paradox: I'm lucky enough that luck plays a slightly less powerful role in my life.

After I pick the fruits, the Guarnizo brothers want to show me the path of the cherry once it has left the tree. We walk a couple of hundred yards to a small shack with a machine the size of a fridge. It's the de-pulper. The cherries are poured into a chute, where they are squished between metal rollers that rip off the skin and flesh.

Out comes a river of slippery white beans, which are dumped into a tub for a couple of days to ferment. The beans are then spread out to dry for about three weeks on a series of mesh screens.

You have to rake the beans to make sure they are drying evenly. Otherwise, the beans could be ruined. In fact, the whole process is extraordinarily delicate. The taste of the coffee can be affected by dozens of variables: the amount of rain, the type of soil, the amount of nitrogen fertilizer. Coffee beans grown in the shade of other trees are smoother-tasting. Even the shape of the piles when drying can alter the flavor—some farmers put them in rows, others build little pyramids.

The coffee faces many threats. There's coffee rust, a fungus, which can spread in a flash. There are the birds that ignore the scarecrows on the mountain, but do fly away when the brothers shoot rifles in the air. The beans that survive are trucked off to a nearby mill, which has machines that separate the beans by color, size, and density.

The brothers offer to take us on a hike up the mountain. We walk along a path, past a machete lying on the ground and a dusty soccer field, then up the steep grade. After fifteen minutes, we stop in a clearing to rest—and to do business.

Here, in perhaps the most beautiful office on earth— tweeting birds, winding trails, deep-green leaves—Ed and Wilmar start discussing the contract, as the other brothers watch intently.

My Spanish is rudimentary, but I get the gist. Wilmar wants

THANKS A THOUSAND 105

to be paid more per pound. Ed is confused because they just signed a three-year contract with an agreed-upon price.

There's no shouting, no stomping, but the atmosphere is quietly tense. Wilmar is pointing out how much work the coffee requires: They have to pick the beans, clean them, dry them. Ed is responding that he's got huge costs: New York rent, shipping, storage.

I'm on the perimeter, awkwardly listening in, unsure whom to agree with. The progressive in me says, of course these men should be paid more. They live on a mountain in South America with no Internet access. They've never traveled outside Colombia, while we just flew in from the U.S. with our iPhones in tow.

But the realist in me argues that Ed already pays them far above fair trade prices. If Ed wanted, he could do business with a bigger, cheaper, more corporate farm and get similar quality beans. Not to mention that Joe Coffee is itself a small business up against Starbucks. Just weeks ago, Ed signed the contract at the price the Guarnizos suggested.

Ed hardly seems like Mr. Monopoly to me. When he told me about the contract a few days ago, he seemed genuinely proud of what he saw as a fair deal that was good to the farmers. He said it was what the farmers preferred, because it guaranteed them money even if the crops were a bust.

I don't know the right answer. I flash back to an article I read a few weeks ago. The idea was that, yes, three dollars for a cup of coffee is ridiculously high. Practically felonious. But if we paid American minimum wage to all the people on the chain, coffee would cost about $25 a cup.

Ed speaks good Spanish but he's not fluent. To avoid any mixed signals, he asks if they can resume the negotiation later, with a translator present. Wilmar and the brothers agree. Both sides take a conciliatory tone. They're sure they'll work something out. (And they do. In fact, weeks later, Ed and the Guarnizos are featured on a coffee blog as a model for business partnerships.)

We come down from the mountain, and the tenseness of the negotiation fades into a friendly lunch at the Guarnizo kitchen table.

Ed takes a spoonful of his chicken soup, brings it to his mouth, and slurps it noisily. We all turn to him. Lorena's eyes are wide with shock and embarrassment.

"*¡Ochenta y ocho!*" Ed declares.

Everyone cracks up.

"*Muy bien,*" says Wilmar's brother Yimmi.

I knew this was coming. Ed had told me that he does the slurping soup joke every year. The idea is that he's rating the soup on the coffee scale—an 88 out of 100. It always works. "It's my only reliable gag," Ed says.

Over lunch, the Guarnizos and I talk about non-coffee topics. I ask about hobbies.

"*Fútbol y bebiendo,*" says Yimmi. Soccer and drinking.

"We don't have much time," Wilmar adds. "I wake up at five thirty in the morning, and am out all day in the fields."

We talk about our health, as middle-aged people around

the world tend to do. Yimmi and I figure out we both had our appendixes removed a couple of years ago. Yimmi pulls up his shirt to show me his scar. It's a big, raised railroad track spreading across his stomach. With first-world guilt, I show him my sliver of a scar.

"*Muy bien,*" he says.

Once again, I realize I'm lucky as hell that I have access to the health care in the United States. And I'm lucky that my wife spent two months navigating the insurance company labyrinth to get most of it covered.

● ● ●

After lunch we have coffee, appropriately enough. We sit on the porch and drink the beverage that Wilmar's wife roasted in a saucepan. It tastes delicious, though perhaps at that altitude, anything would.

Now is the time, I tell myself. Several of the gratitude books I've read suggested writing a gratitude letter and reading it out loud. So, on the plane ride earlier, I'd scribbled my thoughts in syntax-garbled Spanish.

I take out my crumpled piece of loose-leaf paper, look at the Guarnizo family, and read: "*Gracias por ustedes.*"

I continue, in my stumbling Spanish: "I now understand more about all the work that goes into making my morning cup of coffee, and I will not take it for granted again.

"Thank you for picking the beans and washing them and drying them.

"Your coffee has given me great happiness every morning,

and helped give me the energy to write books and articles and take care of my kids.

"From now on, I'll think of you when I drink my morning coffee. And perhaps you will think of people like me in the United States, and the joy you give to us. And perhaps you will think of all the artists and architects and salespeople and engineers in New York who are inspired by what you produce."

I finish. Silence. Not sure there were actual crickets, but I certainly heard some type of buzzing insects.

After a few seconds, I spot Wilmar give just a slightest nod of the head, the faintest hint of a smile.

"Gracias a usted," he says.

I can't say they were ecstatic or transformed, but I'm pretty sure they didn't dislike my thank-you note. So that's something.

As we are leaving, there are handshakes. The Guarnizos invite Ed and me to come next year and stay longer, maybe a couple of nights. I won't take them up on the invitation, but I'm grateful to have it.

It's a week later, and I'm back in New York, six thousand miles from the giant chickens and the cliffside roads of Colombia.

I'm in line for my daily coffee from Joe. I'll soon taste beans whose hometown I've visited. I know the beans won't be impressed, lacking consciousness and all, but it still makes me feel more connected to my drink.

I pick up my cup of coffee and tell the barista, "I'm very grateful for my coffee today."

"As well you should be!" he says. It's become our routine.

I also thank the woman restocking the lids and Java Jackets, as I haven't seen her before.

That makes 964 people I've thanked. Or thereabouts. Unlike the scientific measurements that go into my coffee, my tally isn't exact. I've been keeping a massive list on my computer of names and jobs, but I'm sure there are repeats. There's also some fudging. I recently called a factory in Brazil to say *"obrigado"* for making the de-pulping machines. I asked the factory floor manager to pass along my thanks to the assembly line workers, and I added three more to my total.

On the counter at Joe Coffee there's a photo of one of the farms they work with. It's a nice touch, but I wish there were other photos on the counter too: maybe a photo of the truckers, the dockworkers, the steelworkers, the shipping-container makers; maybe hundreds of people. And maybe a sign that thanks other coffee shops—because coffee fuels thousands of people who make the stuff that helps make my coffee.

This struck me during one of my final interviews. It was with a Minneapolis engineer involved in the forging of the steel that's in trucks, brewing machines, and so much else necessary for my favorite drink.

I asked him, over the phone, "What are you grateful for?"

"I'm grateful for this chair that my fat ass is sitting on," he said.

I laughed. "What kind of chair is it?"

"I'm too lazy to get up and look."

"Fair enough," I said. "Anything else you're grateful for?"

"Well, I'm grateful to coffee. I mean, if you do your book right, you have to thank the coffee itself. Because the steel-workers drink a lot of coffee."

I loved his point. So meta, so recursive, and so true. You need coffee to make coffee. Coffee begets coffee.

A couple of weeks later my phone chimes. It's a text from Chung, the friendliest barista in the world. She's moved to California, but she still texts the occasional hello.

I write back: "My son Zane pointed out that I should thank the parents of those who got me coffee, since they wouldn't be there without their parents. So can you please thank your parents for me?"

By thanking Chung's parents, I've broken a thousand thanks . . . more or less. Could be 987, could be 1,015, but I'm counting it as the thousandth, since it seems tidy.

Chung texts back a series of emojis and exclamation points. "Please tell Zane thank you. And thank you to you both for making me think more about all that I should be grateful for in my life." She says she's thankful for the sacrifices her parents made as immigrants. She says that after our talk, she's realized gratitude is a discipline that needs to be practiced. It doesn't always come naturally, even to glass-half-full types like her.

Chung's texts make me smile like one of the emojis she just sent. Today, I've been happy, or at least non-grumpy, for more than half the day—which makes me grateful.

Not long after, my own parents invite us to dinner at their apartment in honor of my approaching birthday. After we finish the pizza, the boys bring out the cupcakes and sing happy birthday to me.

This is lovely, of course. But I've been thinking about Zane's advice. He's right. I should really be thanking my own mom, especially on this day. It seems odd that birthday celebrations are all about the kid, when they should really be honoring the mom. The emphasis is askew. I mean, what did I do on that day several decades ago? I came out, I cried, I demanded food, I got a mediocre score on my Apgar. The real hero is my mom. She's the one who had her body dangerously distorted by my infant skull.

"Hey, guys, can you sing to Grandma?" I ask. "I think we should be thanking her. She did all the hard work."

My mom smiles and nods. "That's sweet. And you're right. You weren't easy."

● ● ●

The Gratitude Trails intersect and overlap everywhere. In fact, if you mapped them out, you could probably connect almost anyone in this book to almost anyone else. The lumberjacks provide not just wood for coffee cups, but paper used by the importing company to keep records. We need rubber for the tires on the coffee trucks, but also for the trucks that carry the liquid soap to the scientists who test the water for germs.

There is a beautiful scene from the book *Invisible Cities* by Italo Calvino, and I can't help but recall it now. Calvino wrote a fable of a city where people's apartments are connected by threads. The threads are strung from one apartment and across the street or down the block to another apartment. Each thread represents a different kind of relationship. If the people in the two apartments are blood relatives, the threads are black. If they are in business together, the threads are white. If one is the boss of the other, the threads are gray. Eventually, the threads grow so numerous and thick and multi-shaded, it's impossible to walk through the city.

If we connected the world with threads signifying gratitude, the result would be as thick as a blanket.

ACKNOWLEDGMENTS

A Thousand Thanks

By A.J. Jacobs and Riki Markowitz

Since there was no way to fit a thousand thankees into the text of the book itself, I've collected a thousand names below. This will, I hope, give you a sense of how many people it takes to produce the items in our lives and the people we often take for granted.

The thankees listed are a diverse group. Some have contributions that are obvious (the barista and the farmers). Some are admittedly quite tangential (the folks who make the asphalt for the roads on which the coffee-carrying trucks travel). But my thesis is that the world is woven together by connections. So I wanted to be expansive in my thanks, not restrictive. These folks may be tangential, but they are also, oddly enough, crucial.

The result is a map of my Gratitude Trail. (*Gratitude Trail* is a phrase my friend Priscilla Algava came up with, so thanks to her for that.) I encourage you to follow a gratitude trail of your own. It's a wonderful experience. At least it was for me. I learned a shocking amount and I got all sorts of warm and fuzzy feelings, along with occasional sweats from over-caffeination.

Also, thanks to Riki Markowitz, who is an excellent researcher and coffee enthusiast and helped put this list together.

CHAPTER 1
THE BARISTA AND THE TASTER

1. The **barista** Chung Lee at my local Joe Coffee.

2. Ed Kaufmann, the head **coffee buyer** at Joe Coffee Company.

3. Jonathan Rubinstein, the **founder** of Joe Coffee Company.

4-5. Richard and Alice Rubinstein, **Jonathan's parents who invested** in the very first Joe Coffee shop.

6-11. Other key Joe Coffee staff, including Tim Hinton, **manager** of my local Joe Coffee Company, and Frankie Tin, Brandon Wall, Doug Satzman, Will Hewes, and Jonathan's sister, Gabrielle Rubinstein.

12-15. The employees of Mazzer **coffee grinders**, which ground my coffee beans, including Luca Maccatrozzo, Cristian Cipolotti, Luigi Mazzer, and Mattia Miatto.

16-19. Thunder Group, makers of the **strainer** used at Joe Coffee, including Michael Sklar, Brian Young, Takia Augustine, and Robert Huang.

20-22. The folks at Hario **digital scale for coffee**, including Shin Nemoto, Sakai Hario, and Tagawa Hario.

23-25. The workers at the Specialty Coffee Association, including Don Schoenholt, Spencer Turer, and Kim Elena Ionescu, who organize coffee conventions where Joe Coffee employees find **new supplies**.

26-29. Oxo **kitchen tools**, including Juan Escobar, John DeLamar, Eddy Viana, and Lynna Borden.

30-31. **The developers of the coffee flavor chart**, including Edward Chambers and Rhonda Miller, which coffee tasters use to identify flavor.

32. Ed Kaufmann's **tasting teacher**, Rob Stephen.

33-35. **The manufacturers of the tasting spoon** used by Joe Coffee, including Stephen Wright, Beatrice "Beattie" France, and Ryan May of the W. Wright Cutlery & Silverware company.

36-37. **Pioneers of the cupping procedure** used for tasting coffee Clarence Bickford and B.D. Balart.

38-40. **Developers of the Q Grade test used in tasting coffee** Jean Lenoir, David Guermonprez, and Eric Verdier.

41-42. The makers of the Mudjug **spittoon** used by Ed Kaufmann in tasting the coffee, including Darcy Compton and Garrett Celano.

43-45. Neumann Kaffee Gruppe, which **supplies data on coffee trade** to buyers, including Andres Dicker, Catalina Eikenberg, and Dana Andrews.

46-49. The people at Ikawa coffee sample **grinders,** which grinds small batches for tasting, including O.M. Miles, Philip Schluter, Matyas Tamasi, and Andrew Stordy.

50-52. Workers at **Moleskine notebooks,** which Ed Kaufmann uses to make notes on the coffee tastings, including Alma Ibershimi, Michael Steigman, and Tetsu Nakazawa.

53. There are many people throughout history who helped make coffee a popular beverage, including **Kaldi the goatherd,** the ancient Ethiopian who first discovered coffee (according to legend, anyway). He apparently saw his goats jumping and dancing after eating coffee beans.

54. **Horticulturist** Gabriel de Clieu, French naval officer who apparently planted a seedling in Martinique in the 1720s that is the ancestor of all coffee trees in South America.

55. **Coffee pioneer** Alfred Peet, who introduced high-end coffee to the United States in 1966.

56. **Pope Clement VIII,** who gave papal approval of coffee. "We shall fool Satan by baptizing it and making it a truly Christian beverage."

57-59. **Boston Tea Party participants,** who played a part in making coffee instead of tea the American beverage, including Thompson Maxwell, Obadiah Curtis, and Joseph Coolidge.

60-62. The folks who made it **possible for me to pay** for my coffee, including the staff at **American Express credit cards,** such as Jane Di Leo, Sarah Jukes, and Marci Lowney.

63-65. NXP Semiconductors makes the **computer chip in my credit card** and is staffed by Tate Tran, Dale Eagar, and Metin Onder.

66-69. American National Standards Institute is the group that **makes the numbers for credit cards,** so thanks to Sarah Bloomquist, Petra Valentin, Amama Idrees, and Beth Lisa Adams.

70-72. The folks at Square, the **electronic cash register** that allowed me to pay for my coffee, including Julie Kerner, Amy Feitelberg, and Mallory Russell.

73-76. AtLite makes the emergency **lighting at Joe Coffee,** so thanks to employees Michael Jacobs, Liz Gimondo, Ricky James, and Russell Tatum.

77–80. The folks who help make the CMA **dishwasher at Joe Coffee**, including Grace Petit, Emily Dominguez, Mohit Ahuja, and Kristian Fedri.

81–84. The people at Buckeye Fire Equipment, which makes the **fire extinguisher at Joe Coffee** so that it can stay open, including Jack Julian, Bryon Gordon, Joey Word, and Mike Patti.

85–88. The workers at John Boos & Co., which makes the **sink at Joe Coffee**, including Tom Murphy, Tony Kemme, Garland Gibson, and David Weatherman.

89–92. The employees of Norpak Corporation, which makes **deli paper** used at Joe Coffee, Lydia Matas, Dale Song, Andrew Crumrine, and Michele Guddemi.

93–95. **True Refrigerators**, used by Joe Coffee to keep milk cold, has staffers including Rick Gengaro, Bob Trulaske, and Art Trulaske.

96. Also, thanks to the **inventor of refrigeration**, Jacob Perkins.

97–99. The people at Kobalt tools, which makes the **air compressor at Joe Coffee**, including Kimber Biniak Jones, Jonathan Bradshaw, and Eduardo Gonzalez.

100–103. The employees of **Everpure water purifier** used by Joe Coffee, including Rick Rounds, Anthony Critelli, Frank Kernan, and Devin Hare.

104–107. Eaton Cutler-Hammer, makers of the **power outlets at Joe Coffee** that power the grinders that make my coffee, including Vernon Young, Anthony Wilson, Christopher Kaiser, and Maria Morla.

108–111. The folks at Toto **toilets**, installed at Joe Coffee so that the employees can follow nature's calls, including May Tang, Christian Rowe, Peter Stangel, and Micah Tice.

112. Shawn, who does **plumbing** work at Joe Coffee.

113–116. NuTone, makers of the **ventilation fans at Joe Coffee**, including John Stafford, Darshit Gosalia, Eshank Singh, and Priyanka Pillai.

117–120. The people at Werner Co., which makes the **ladder at Joe Coffee** that the workers use to get the coffee from storage, including Chad Lingerfelt, Dan Mora, Mike Katz, and Jason Scott.

121–124. Gleason Corp., maker of the **hand trucks used to move bags at Joe Coffee**, including Jennifer Schweitzer, Harsh Pandya, Jim Adams, and Rayford Callicutt.

125–128. Glidden Professional, makers of the **sealer used in the Joe Coffee kitchen**, including Thomas Biggs, Juan Maldonado, Al Groff Jr., and Hal Horn.

129–132. Benjamin Moore & Co., **makers of the paint for the walls at Joe Coffee**, including Bonnie Sachinis, Julia Kremen, Eileen McComb, and Megan Cangialosi.

133–136. The folks who make the **modular container** for **Joe Coffee** at Iris USA, including Kevin Kissell, Derrick Reed, Patrick Gorman, and Natalie Quinnies.

137–140. The coffee supplies are stored on Nexel **wire shelving**, so thanks to Donald McKenna, Jennifer Tallon-Diglio, Anthony Carrotta, and Kevin Chow.

141–144. Joe Coffee supplies are also stored in **bags** from Ikea, so thanks to Steve LaVictoire, Jon Evoy, Cherisse Jeffries, and Donald Acton.

145–148. The people at Homz, makers of the **plastic boxes** where coffee is stored at Joe Coffee, including Nicole Guenther, Stan Borione, Peter Spratt, and Daniel Bartlett.

149–153. Stanley **milk containers** from Pacific Market International, including Dana Kohlmann, Kathlyn Jones, Judy Burke, Lisa Wood, and Mike Pietrowski.

154–156. **Sugar In The Raw** employees, including Kate Schneider, Les Dessources, and Sara Hoskow.

157–160. The makers of **office supplies** for Joe Coffee, including Canon USA, who manufactures the printer at Joe Coffee, including Chuck Westfall, Jerry Karp, Michael Thompson, and Lawrence Davis.

161–164. Staples, which makes the **calculator** used at Joe Coffee to figure out my coffee's pricing and inventory, including Jason Oliver, Lewis Tse, Josh Kindberg, and Brian Katz.

165–168. Ed uses BIC **pens** to take notes on the coffees, so thanks to Emily Hogan, Jim Reel, Johanne Henderson, and Emily Elms.

169–172. UPS, which is used by Joe Coffee for **business shipping**, including employees Quadir Hameed, Franny Hughes, Chuck Astor, and Jason Jimenez.

173–174. Oh, and the **parents of my barista** Chung Lee.

CHAPTER 2
THE CUP MAKERS

175-179. **Cup sleeve makers** Jay Sorensen, Cari L'abbe, Clem Harris, Bill Wadhams, and Colleen Sorensen at Java Jacket, the company that invented the finger-protecting cardboard coffee cup sleeve.

180-182. The folks at Vaporpath, **makers of the Viora Lid coffee cup lid**, Barry Goffe, Cloantha Copass, and Doug Fleming.

183. **Coffee cup lid pioneer** Alan Frank.

184-188. **Manufacturers of paper cups** at Imperial Dade, including Robert Tillis, Jason Tillis, Jameka Carter, Rick Tabit, and David Pokorny.

189-192. **Staff at International Paper**, which distributes paper for the cups, including Sean James, Jimenez George, Clifton Moore, and Shane Kelleher.

193-194. Domtar **pulp mill, which makes paper for the coffee cups**, including Paul Kallioinen and Thomas Looney.

195-198. **Paper cup inventors** Lawrence Luellen and Austin Pinkham, who were distressed by health hazards of drinking from common water buckets, invented the Health Kup in 1907, one of the first paper cups. Other coffee cup pioneers were Michael Brillis and Pollick Frank.

199-203. Charles Fenerty, Friedrich Gottlob Keller, J. Roth, Henry Voelter, and Cai Lun **invented the wood pulp process for papermaking**.

204-207. Joe Coffee **logo designers**, including Marke Johnson, Amber Chiarelli, Adam Blake, and Kimberly Johnson at the Made Shop.

208. **Type inventor** Alex Haigh, designer of the Nanami font used in the logo.

209-211. **Adobe software for designing** the logo, including Gerald Farro, Brenda Milis, and Fiona Gardner.

212-217. **The developers of the plastic used to coat the inside of the cups**: Jöns Jacobs Berzelius, Edmond Williams and Richard Shappell, Alexander Parkes, Leo Baekland, and Jacques Edwin Brandenberger.

218. Franklin Moss **invented the Flexo Printing method** used by Java Jacket.

219-220. **Inventors of screen-printing technique used in cups**, including Samuel Simon and Michael Vasilantone.

221. **Barcode maker** Advantage Technology Solutions staff, including Frank Angotti, used for coffee supplies.

222–226. Kice makes **dust control air systems** for plastic makers; staff includes Tom Zemanick, Doyle Hamilton, Jeff Kice, Katy Lamb, and Les Brin.

227. The **inventor of corrugated cardboard** used in packaging the cups, Albert Jones.

228–230. Lamitech, provider of cardboard **boxes**, including Tim Pocock, Andrew Londergan, and Jerry Sarno.

CHAPTER 3
THE ROASTERS

231–232. Amaris Gutierrez-Ray and Roberta Durate, **roasters** at Joe Coffee.

233–236. Staff at Extech, makers of the **meter that measures water density in the beans**, Haley Ellison, Luciane McCarthy, Teri King, and Michael Oster.

237–239. Joe Coffee **packers** including Lee Harrison, Eric Heredia, and Vlad Kanevsky.

240–242. The folks at GrainPro bags, **specialty plastic bags for shipping coffee**, Jose Gomez, Joey Saligao, and Diego Lara Lavarreda.

243–246. Pacific Bag, which makes **consumer coffee bags** for coffee shops, including Adrienne Rummerfield, Jui Chen "Charlene" Fang, Katie Farrell, and Christopher Mitchell.

247–249. Rubbermaid, makers of the **bins used to store coffee**, including Homayoun Khalili, Rita Hunter, and Blake Bodie.

250–255. The people at Cropster **software for coffee roasters**, Norbert Niederhauser, Taylor Wallace, Andreas Idl, Martin Wiesinger, Laura Liivo, and Michelle Hasbrouck.

256–258. Atago, **makers of acidometers** to test coffee beans, including Tayler Stevens, Emerson Carillo, and Carla Julio.

259–261. Those who work at **Ziploc bags, used for storing coffee**, including Brian Tippett, Marcelo Stefani, and Jacqueline Holliday.

262–263. **Designers of the plastic zipper** used on Ziploc bags, Borge Madsen and Max Ausnit.

264-267. Loring coffee **roaster manufacturers** Tina Williams, Joshua Hutton, Robert Disidoro, and Mark Ludwig.

268-270. The Joe Coffee roasters (and much of the rest of the staff) use Apple computers to keep track of inventory and order new coffee. Among those who make Apple computers possible are Coilcraft, which makes **coils for Apple computers** used at Joe Coffee, including John Neumann, Jacob Klein, and Madhavi Polisetti.

271-275. Knowles makes **audio parts for Apple computers**, including Dennis Marcotte, Hassan Dani, Denis Loxha, Robert Fabian McCarthy, and Brandon Peeler.

276-280. Infineon Technologies makes **semiconductors** for Apple computers, including Steve Bakos, Christian Becker, Shrikant Joshi, Mario Campello, and Stephanie Garcia.

281-285. Qualcomm worked on **3G for Apple** computers, including Nate Tibbits, Jeff Arouh, Navaneetha Krish, Chakravarthy Madirafu, and Khaled El-Maleh.

286-290. Kyocera makes **precision cutting tools** out of carbide that Apple uses to make computers, including Michael Ward, Jim Doughty, Gary Miller, Steve Chochrane, and James Loso.

291-295. Nan Ya Plastics Corporation USA makes **synthetic fiber** used in Apple computers, including Robert Peng, Henry Liao, Max Peng, Dung-yi Chao, and Paul Stanzione.

296-298. Cheng Loong Corp., which provides **printing paper** for offices, Wei-Lun Chang, Billy Tu, and Ken Nelson.

299-300. Radiant Opto-Elect technology, **LED display manufacturer**, including Chewei Chang and Yong Zhu.

301-305. Prent Corp. makes **packaging for computers**, so thanks to Anthony Cass, Donald Lehr, Haydn Wolff, Jacob Gray, and Laura Collins.

306-308. Platinum Optics Technology, **maker of glass for computers**, Jean-Bernard Bouche, Hsiang Wei Hsieh, and Chien-Liang Liu.

309-313. POSCO, **steel maker for Apple** computers, including Jinseok Hwang, Sangwoo Park, Seung Joon Lee, Elizabeth Pickens, and Steven Bigatti.

314-318. Primax Electronics makes **cameras for computers** and smartphones, Matt Severaid, Martha Elliott, Alexander Lee, Charles Yang, and Robert Tsai.

319-323. Qorvo, which makes **sound technology for Apple**, John Carlson, David Shih, Carla Susmilch, Jason Womack, and Thi Ri Mya Kywe.

324–326. Amkor Technology, which does **semiconductor testing**, including Erin Cote Martin, JaeTaek Yoo, and Kwangmo "Chris" Lim.

327–331. KibbeChem makes **colors for plastics** that are found in Apple products, including Rick Mann, Shannon Rice, Dan Roeske, Shane Kibbe, and Dave Ward.

332. Tim Berners-Lee, one of the inventors of **the World Wide Web**.

333. Ernest Earl Lockhart, researcher who **discovered people prefer coffee that's been brewed between 194 and 205° F.**

334. Ramin Narimani, employee at Pulley Collective, the **industrial space** where Joe Coffee leases space for its roasting operation.

335–337. Those who work at Mahlkönig **coffee bean grinders**, including Moritz von Stietencron, Timo Keimer, and Oliver Bradshaw.

338. J-Scale, the **scale that weighs coffee beans**, with Cimmerian Coleman.

339–342. The Mierisch family, including Doc, Erwin and Eleane, who own a coffee farm in Nicaragua and whose son Steve **opened the Pulley Collective**, where Joe Coffee is roasted.

CHAPTER 4
THE WATER

343–346. Thermo Fisher Scientific, **makers of the ovens** used in testing the water, Alan Polonsky, Lisa Hayes, Amanda Wilson, and Marc Casper.

347–348. **Police that protect the NYC water source** reservoir, including Sean Dewey and Anthony Glorioso.

349–354. **Coleman coolers**, where samples from the reservoir are stored, including Tricia Hyde, Lori Becker, Eileen Litchy, Logan Groves, Jennifer Karbs, and Kevin Beerman.

355–361. Makers of **Cabela's waterproof suits** for the workers who test the water in the reservoirs, including Bob Getz, Ilona Luja, James Pickinpaugh, Stephanie Miller, Chris Fletcher, Scott Williams, and Thomas Milner.

362–365. Makers of **Pyrex used in bottles** in the water testing lab, Anne Moser, Ambyre Balut, Michael Scheffki, and Missy Stefanik.

366-371. Pall Corporation, makers of **bottles used for filtration** tests, including Rick Mumley, Naresh Podila, Rachel Gambetta, Suzanne Hennings, Kelly Bebee, and Siavash Darvishmanesh.

372. Adam Bosch, who does **communications** for the New York City water system.

373. Mark Dubois, who **monitors the reservoirs** for New York water.

374. Kristen Askildsen, a **chemist at the reservoir** that provides water to New York City.

375-378. Others at the **Department of Environmental Protection who oversee the reservoirs,** including Andrew Kuchynsky, Garfield Carty, Thomas Wise, and Jim Pynn.

379-383. General Foundries, which makes **the water testing stations** in New York streets, Sam Chowdhuri, Alok Todani, Ajay Narang, Vinoth Vasu, and Rajiv Sachdev.

384. Theodor Escherich **discovered *E. coli*,** which the EPA tests our water for.

385. Washington Senator Warren Magnuson, who **introduced the Safe Drinking Water Act**.

386. John Snow, **safe water pioneer,** discoverer of cholera transmission in nineteenth-century London.

387-390. The folks at Hach, makers of **water testing equipment**, Pat Lawrence, Kevin Klau, Fern Kidder, and Clifford Hach.

391-392. Thermmax, makers of **walk-in humidity-controlled rooms** for water testing, including Jack Halloran and Kevin Murray.

393. Waldo Semon, **inventor of PVC,** used for water distribution pipes.

394-396. Workers at Georgia-Pacific, which makes **paper towels** used at the reservoir lab, and at Joe Coffee itself, including Phil Garrison, Nick Selissen, and Cathy Robertson.

397-398. **Builders of Tunnel No. 3,** the tunnel that brings water to New York City, including Martin Hauptman and John Gluszak.

CHAPTER 5
THE SAFETY PATROL

399–401. Cintas **first aid kits** to keep steelworkers safe, Elizabeth Quinn, Nicholas Siljee, and Robert Dale Ledbetter.

402. Dr. Harvey W. Wiley, a **drafter of the Pure Food and Drug Act**.

403. President Theodore Roosevelt, who signed and **passed the Pure Food and Drug Act.**

404–407. **Researchers who show coffee has health benefits,** such as delaying dementia, including Neal Freedman, Francesco Panza, Harris Lieberman, and Charles Reed.

408–410. **Makers of sewage and water pumps** Gorman-Rupp, including Tim Cline, Larry Madeker, and Todd Wise.

411. Alexander Cruikshank Houston developed **chlorine** used in water to prevent typhoid.

412–415. **U.S. customs and import specialists** Angela Vitale, Marie Andujar, Catherine Giarraputo-Saluccio, and Steven Welch at U.S. Customs and Border Protection.

416. Amanda Tripple, **dog trainer for agriculture at U.S. Customs and Border Protection.**

417–418. New York **elected officials** overseeing Joe Coffee zoning, including Helen Rosenthal and Gale Brewer.

419–421. Corinne Schiff, **deputy commissioner of New York City Department of Health and Mental Hygiene,** as well as others at the health department, including Seth Guthartz, Mary Bassett, and Emiko Otsubo.

422–426. The Occupational Safety and Health Administration, which **oversees the safety** of Joe Coffee workers, including Michael Yarnell, Cindy Piest, Laura Kenny, Jose Caraballo, and Rick Gray.

427–429. There are lots of people who help keep Joe Coffee sanitary, including the staff at **Mrs. Meyer's hand soap,** which Joe Coffee shop uses to keep baristas' hands clean, including Pam Helms, Thelma Meyer, and Katie Anderson.

430–433. People at **Mr. LongArm, the mop** used to keep Joe Coffee clean, including Melodie Wendleton, Jessica Johnson, Brenda Adkins, and R.D. Newman.

434-436. **The City of New York Department of Sanitation** workers, who clear garbage from Joe Coffee, Daniel Allende, Belinda Edwards, and Cornell Kelly.

437-440. North Shore Linen employees, **responsible for washing the aprons** for the Joe Coffee baristas: Gary Brooks, Larry Gentile, Nicholas Tsiokos, and Heydi Herrera.

441-444. Urnex **coffee equipment cleaning products**, including Jamil Al Asri, Ed Saar, Maarten van der Loop, and Andrea Eigel.

445-448. Makers of Seventh Generation **cleaning liquid**, used for sanitizing Joe Coffee, including Lara Petersen, Jerica Young, Martin Wolf, and Matt Bertonica.

449-452. Bar Keepers Friend, **polisher used at Joe Coffee**, Nidia Ríos, Genni Russell, Matthew Selig, and Kenneth Newton Walker.

453-455. Workers who make and market Fab **detergent, used to clean the coffee cups** at the Colombia processing plant, including Madeline Szul, Matthew Leung, and Matthew Kronengold.

456-462. Glad **garbage bags**, including employees Cecilia Melby, Matthew Bull, Michael Costello, and Khorshid Rahmaninejad. As well as **garbage bag pioneers** Larry Hansen, Harry Wasylyk, and Frank Plomp.

463-466. The people at Kness Manufacturing, which makes the Ketch-All **mousetrap at Joe Coffee**, including Scott Vestal, Jessica Montegna-Terry, Misty Little, and Jonathan Beltz.

467-468. Carefree **Janitorial Supply**, including Joe Roussel and Mark Braswell.

469-472. Agion **antimicrobial steel coating for the sink**, including Jason Fuller, Danielle Bales, Craig Tuttle, and Will Johnson.

CHAPTER 6

THE MOVERS

473-478. Folks at **Continental Terminals coffee warehouse**, where the coffee is stored, including Jackie Massamillo, Andy Turkowitz, Jessica Garcia, Raymond Hutchinson, Bob Forcillo, and Dan Marsling.

479-481. Insulated **curtain walls for warehouses** from Randall Manufacturing, including Anna Prokopowicz, Michael Galati, and Jian Jiang.

482-483. Parkway Pest Services, **pest control for the warehouse**, including Peter Scala and Shoshanah Howell.

484-488. Hughes Enterprises, makers of **strapping for pallets**, Amy Packer, Neal Magaziner, Stan Auerbach, Vanessa Linder, and Cynthia Kolczynski.

489-490. **Inventors of the wooden pallet**, William House and George Raymond.

491-493. Decker Tape Product, which makes **tape for boxes and shipping**, including Noreen Smith, Tim Rolfes, and Jack Decker.

494-496. There are tons of folks involved in trucking my coffee, including Accurate Logistics **trucking company** employees Kenny Monaco, Maria Del Vals, and trucker Miguel Rosas.

497-501. Freightliner **truck-maker**, including Leland James, Jason Wright, David Carson, Kelly Gedert, and James Sheridan.

502-504. Makers of Swig Savvy **water bottles, used by the truckers** who haul Joe Coffee, including Yan Izrailov, Grant Gilbert, and Bob Gilbert.

505-508. Magna makes **fuel valves for cars and trucks**, and includes Eddie Snipes, Nicolas Shaya, John Ralston, and Malika Patricia Hunt.

509-511. Delphi makes **parts for fuel economy and emissions** in trucks and cars, and includes Aravindhan Ramesh, Rajesh Pokala, and Shradha Sharma.

512-514. Husco International makes **fluid-related parts for cars and trucks**, and includes Winny Chanthalalay, Todd Murray, and Benjamin Beyer.

515-517. Inalfa Roof Systems makes **roofs for cars and trucks**, and includes Rick Braun, Jorge Olivera, and Karen Ramos.

518-520. IAC Group makes **trim and moldings for cars and trucks**, and includes John Rose, Herman Alston, and Jubal Feazell.

521-523. Kautex Textron makes **fuel tanks for cars and trucks**, and includes Janeth Valdez, Alexander Bronk, and Nicolle Anderson.

524-527. Kiekert makes **door latches for cars and trucks**, and includes Mark Smith, Ujwal Velagapudi, Hector Verde, and Mark Krzesak.

528-531. Lear Corporation makes **nameplates for cars and trucks**, and includes Carlos Monzon, Barbara Boroughf, Krystal Brown, and Osvaldo Sanchez.

532-535. Linamar Corporation makes **axles for cars and trucks**, and includes Hoang Huynh, Matthew Lajcak, Tre Ledbetter, and Nicole Grein.

536–539. Goodyear employees make the **truck tires**, and include Jon Bellissimo, Sidney Richardson, Frank Seiberling, and Lucius Miles.

540. Charles Goodyear, **inventor of vulcanized rubber used in tires** on the trucks that haul the coffee.

541. Robert William Thompson, **Scottish engineer who first patented the air-filled tire**.

542. Senator Al Gore Sr. helped pass the **Federal-Aid Highway Act of 1956** that created interstate highways.

543–546. Staff at Morgan, which makes the **bodies for the trucks** used in transporting coffee bags, Elton Mountz, Corby Stover, Ryan Shirk, and Frank Maldonado.

547–549. Staff at Adient, which makes **seating for cars and trucks**, Lewis Murphy Schiavon, Venkat Chenna, and Raul Pinillos.

550–552. Axalta, **manufacturer of liquid coatings for cars**, with Victor D'Ascenzo, Arun Surendranath, and Gaurang Bhargava.

553–555. Detroit Thermal Systems, making **climate control parts for cars and trucks**, including Donald Dahl, Ali Farhat, and James Ezuruonye.

556–558. Dicastal North America, **makers of aluminum alloy wheels**, including Yuqian Wang, Xingye Dai, and Steve Eichbauer.

559–561. The staff at Autoliv, which manufactures **car and truck safety parts**, Chaimae Najime, Brendan Fonte, and Aaron Schaal.

562–566. Mann+Hummel, makers of **air filters for cars**, including Samuel Kline, Jim Screnci, Allayne Washington, Tara Grisolia, and Justin Oldani.

567–571. Martinrea, makers of **fuel and brake lines**, including Dylan Bing, Lance Conyne, Sean Peterson, Tyangela Crawford, and Rushabh Patel.

572–574. AGC Asahi Glass, which makes **glass for cars and trucks**, Yuji Yamamoto, Masahide Yodogawa, and Fernando Garcia.

575–577. Federal-Mogul Motorparts, **windshield wiper manufacturer**, including Joe Dunn, Anthony Serrecchia, and Dan Mirocco.

578–580. Flex-N-Gate, **headlamp supplier**, with Mark Griswold, Brent Langley, and Ryan MacDonald.

581–583. Akebono, makers of **noise and vibration solutions for brakes** in cars, including Sai Chand, Maria Page, and Mykhaylo "Mike" Kovalenko.

584-586. **Automotive Lighting** company for cars and trucks, including Deepak Sahu, Stacie Covey, and Eduardo Escalera.

587-591. NEAPCO, which makes **drive shafts for trucks**, including Bill Podbutzky, Keith Rissell, Paul Roman, Marie Kauffman, and Don Mitchell.

592-596. Nemak, which provides **lightweight cylinder heads**, including Jon Garcia, Dickey Randy, Yates Daniel, Rick Hardin, and Lomas Alejandro.

597-601. Nexteer Automotive, **steering technology**, Tim Kaufmann, Paula Lin, Kevin Weber, Jim Czolgosz, and Miguel Moreno.

602-606. Rheinmetall Group, **provides emissions technology for trucks and cars**, including Ganesh Subramanian, Ron Waltemate, Olaf Tews, Vikrant Rayate, and Mika Nuotio.

607-611. Mubea, which makes **suspension coil springs**, including Giorgio Fiore, Patricia Rodriguez, John Davidson, Andrew Andersen, and Ramkumar Annadurai.

612-637. The twenty-six workers (carpenters, stone layers, foremen) who died while **building the Brooklyn Bridge**, either by drowning, the bends, collapsing materials, etc., including Charles Young, John French, Thomas Talbot, John Deneys, Patrick McKay, John Meyers, Daniel Reardon, John Enright, Cornelius McLaughlin, Lourtz Hensen, Peter Koop, William Reid, John Elliott, William Cambridge, Neil Mullen, Henry Supple, Thomas Blake, Michael Noone, Patrick Murphy, Thomas Martin, Michael Collins, William Delaney, E.F. Farrington, Arthur Abbott, William Van der Bosch, and Harry Supple. The bridge is used by trucks to deliver coffee.

638-639. **New York City Department of Transportation**, in charge of highways and roads, including Polly Trottenberg and Bob Collyer.

640. **New York State Bridge Authority**, in charge of bridges, including Richard Gerentine.

641-643. **Asphalt Drum Mixers** staff, including Brandon Cox, Braxton Powers, and Carlos Cardenas.

644-646. Astec Industries, manufacturer of **equipment for road building**, including Wes Berg, Quinn Gable, and Hoyt Grimes.

647-649. Eisenwerk Brühl, maker of **cylinder blocks** used in road building, including Timm Ziehm, Wilm Papke, and Kevin Caldwell.

650-652. Bomag, maker of **machines that compact asphalt**, including Jim Head, Christopher Fannin, and Tom Scalla.

653. Kenneth Ingalls Sawyer, developer of the **center line on highways** for traffic safety.

654-655. Pioneers of **paving and cement** used in highways, including George Bartholomew and Joseph Aspdin.

656-660. Zimmerman Paint Contractors, **paint the striping on highways**, including Brandon Willer, Bill Sheets, Jack Zimmerman, Lorraine Zimmerman, and Liz Peck.

661-663. Foreverlamp, designers of **lamps for highways**, including Lavina Correia, Ray Hsu, and Nisen Zhang.

664-665. Anpeng Wire Mesh Filter Co., equipment **for asphalt creations**, including Sunny Wu and Rosa Cao.

666-669. Sylvania **light bulbs that are used in traffic signals** on the roads the trucks use, Jocelyn Wensel, Jonathan Hoffman, Michael Anderson, and Daryl Kanatzar.

670-674. Tenneco makes **valves for trucks,** and includes Kim Blalock, Ryan Roeber, Jay Larouche, Kim Yapchai, and Fei Fei Metzler.

675. John Jurgeleit of the Maspeth Central Shop, where **New York City street signs** are made.

676-678. **Software for road construction**, Kespry, including Brian Isbell, Jim Allison, and Jason Nichols.

679-681. Eagle Crusher Company, **makers of portable crushers for roads and asphalt**, including Troy Meadows, Tim Ursich, and Robyn Beal.

682-684. **Quality Pavement Repair** staff, including Cindy Richard, Shaina DeStefano, and Emmanuel Contreras.

685-687. Those at Sakai, makers of **rollers to pave roads**, including Mike Mercer, Jamie Holbert, and Kendall Phillips.

688-711. Shipping my coffee takes a huge number of folks, including the Hong Kong Express **ship crew**, which brings the coffee to the port, including **officers, electricians, cooks, and engineers** such as Ariel Agalla, John Ryan Consad, Generoso Caneja, Angelito Segundino, Cesar Escobal, Maurice Bajo, Christoph Heers, Günter Naborowski, Ansgar Lehmköster, Danilo Napoto, Pawel Sobolewski, Aivan Delgado, John Aumüller, Lasse Gawande, Uriel Lumanog, Juan Carlos Nirza, Jay Vee Cruz, Mac Lawrence Dadivas, Remar Locsin, Genadij Dubrow, Gabriel Yana, Rheinell Nolasco, Michael Nierra, and Yonger Chaux.

712. Robert Watson-Watt, **developer of first practical radar system for ships**.

713-715. Maersk **shipping line**, including Brionna Sanders, An Lam, and Kalliopi Pahountis.

716–718. Øglænd System, **makers of ladders for ships**, including Martine Malde, Louis LeBourgeois, and Kai-Lee Chang.

719–721. Eupec makes **coating for pipes on ships** that haul coffee, Nicolas Hersent, Bruno Brément, and Nathalie Verove.

722. Scarecrow bio-acoustic systems, makers of equipment that **scares off birds** from marine areas for ships, Katie Wells.

723–725. Pharos Marine Automatic Power, Inc., **makers of radar beacons** for ships, including Rene "Boogie" LeBlanc, Tom Lamb, and Beau O'Quin.

726–728. COMP-Air Service, **makers of air compressors used to store air needed to start ship engines**, including Tony Montalto, Mario Bardelas, and Miguel Angel Cardenas.

729–731. DNV-GL, marine warranty survey, doing **safety checks on ships** that carry the coffee, Luis D'Angelo, Joseph Lopes, and Sander Wielemaker.

732–734. Maze Nails makes **nails for building ports**, Len Kasperski, Chadd Kreofsky, and Roelif Loveland.

735–736. Jorm Springer and Henri Scheer, providers of **weather reports** to ships carrying coffee.

737–739. Hemisphere, sellers of **commercial satellite positioning** products for shipping, Max DeForest, David Maurer, and Michael Troidl.

740–742. **GPS co-inventors** including Ivan Getting, Bradford Parkinson, and Roger Easton.

743–744. Inventor of **metal shipping container**, Malcom McLean. And James Brindley, of the wooden precursor.

745–746. Daewoo **Shipbuilding & Marine Engineering** staff, including Yu Chang Lim and Seung Jae Hong.

747–749. Real Safety **anti-slip stickers** used in shipping, Iman Aref, Lise Løth Nielsen, and Mahammad Hossein Forouzbakhsh.

750–752. Florens **container leasing**, including Peter Su, Winnie Siu, and Li Guomei.

753–755. Ports America, which operates the **port where the coffee comes in**, including Eric Soler, Stephen Kovacs, and Katja Loughman.

756–758. The Port Authority of New York and New Jersey, which **oversees the New York ports**, including Kevin O'Toole, D. Austin Futch, and Mervin Horst.

759–761. Terex, makers of **container-moving machines**, Brian Hurley, Tony Rust, and Stephen Johnston.

762–767. The coffee is carried from Colombia in boats, but much of the business is done by airplanes. Including Avianca, the **Colombian airline** that coffee buyer Ed Kaufmann takes to get to the farm, including pilots, flight attendants and ticketing agents such as Alejandra Valentin, Octavio Sandoval, Maiky Alexandra Joya-Kuffer, Diego Garrido Morales, Paola Guzman, and Andres Osorio.

768–769. **Airplane manufacturer** Airbus, which makes the planes that take buyer Ed Kaufmann to Colombia, including Thomas Enders and Franz Josef Strauss.

770–773. El Dorado **airport employees in Bogotá, Colombia**, including Susana Vargas Herrán, Alina Sepulveda, Ricardo Naranjo, and Angela Paola Fonseca Uribe.

774–781. **Caravela Coffee importers** for Joe Coffee, who deal with customs and logistics, including Badi Bradley, Anthony Auger, Christy Wicker, Matt Kolb, James Gibbs, Daniel Bolivar, Lorena Falla, and Alejandro Cadena.

782–786. There are many other forms of transportation involved, including the **subways that brought Chung** the barista to Joe Coffee. So thanks to the Metropolitan Transit Authority, including Judith Charles, Joy Moy, James Heckstall, Cecilia Brown, and Jody Johnson.

787–791. Amadeus Rail IT Systems, makes **software for subways**, Franck Vandenbroucke, Ilia Kostov, Valérian Roche, Florian Maupas, and Roy Goldschmitt.

792–795. Kawasaki Heavy Industries, Sheena Angra, Dave Cadamuro, Patrick Petroff, and Tex Sanada, makers of **New York subway cars**.

796–799. Craftsman, which **makes the toolbox** used in the factory making subway cars, Ian Buxton, Jamie Danskin, Julie Wright, and Jamie Matthews.

800–803. Macton Corporation, **makes turntables used in the subway manufacturing plant**, Timothy Brenes, Ryan Knapp, Andy Barry, and Tom Taylor.

804–805. Massimo Vignelli and Bob Noorda, who designed **the New York subway** color-coded circles.

806–809. The people at Bianchi USA, which makes the **bike that Ed Kaufmann uses to get to Joe Coffee** to taste my coffee, including Will Mahler, Erin Kocab, William Potter, and Juan Ortiz.

810–811. The daily prices for the beans at the co-op are written on a whiteboard, so thanks to Albert Stallion and Jerry Woolf for inventing the **whiteboard** and erasable marker.

CHAPTER 7
THE EXTRACTORS

812–814. Makers of Bullard **hardhats, used in mining**, Wells Bullard, Matthew King, and Josh Haldeman.

815. Immanuel Nobel, **inventor of the tool used to make plywood**, used in floors and roofing.

816–818. Royal 4 Systems, makers of **conveyer belt software**, including Isaac Lichtenfeld, Tighe Reardon, and Kim Gregory Emond.

819–821. Bulldog Battery Corporation, manufacturers of **industrial batteries**, including Al Rutledge, Walter Benjamin, and Randy Duly.

822–824. Cat **forklift makers** including Hoa Tran, Gregory Foster, and Anghelov Medina.

825–828. National Grid, **providers of gas** for the company that cleans Joe Coffee's linens, including Dean Seavers, Huascar Ozoria, William Waters, and Darryl Miller.

829–831. Con Edison, **suppliers of electricity** to Joe Coffee, including Craig Mayer, Brian Manzino, and George Loria.

832–834. Watson Adventures, which does **team-building events** for Con Ed and others, including Bret Watson, Stacy King, and Rachel Duncan. (Okay, I know this is more of a stretch than some others, but it's my wife's company and I couldn't resist including it.)

835–839. Matheson supplies the **argon gas for light bulbs**, and includes John Bigham, Mike Babyak, Junko Lindberg, Scott Duff, and Kapil Gupta.

840–842. **Makers of mining equipment** Ray Szwec, Paul Borbely, and Andy Jackson.

843–845. Cleveland-Cliffs, **miners who provide iron ore** that's turned into steel for coffee-making appliances, including Patrick Bloom, Daniel Bilewicz, and Steve Pause.

846. Archie Coburn, **mine safety** federal inspector.

847–849. Aqua Power makes **batteries used in iron mining**, Leila Elhansali, Bala Chandran, and Odd Arild Hovland.

850–852. Carmeuse Lime and Stone provides **lime for steel**, Christopher Seabolt, Levi Weathermon, and Keith Acker.

853–855. Workers at Conn-Weld Industries, who make **screens used for mining**, including Marvin Woodie, Anthony Fink, and William Jones.

856–860. The people at ArcelorMittal, **makers of steel** used in trucks to transport the coffee and kitchen appliances, including Michael Velez, Tracey Lester, Nicholas West, Jolice Pojeta, and Dena Adams.

861–863. American Engineering Testing, which **tests steel equipment**, including Art Johnson, John Haupt, and Roger Hodson.

864–866. Berry Metal Company, which sells **parts for steel furnaces**, Bob Barthelemy, Andrea Davis, and Edward Green.

867–869. ASKO, which makes **knives for cutting steel**, Amy Mallinger, Michael Simko, and David Robertson.

870–872. Alter Trading, **metal recycling**, Robert Husske, Dan Berman, and Ricky McGee.

873–875. Allgaier Process Technology, **machines for washing industrial parts**, Michelle Bennett, Monica Bonner, and Mark London.

876–877. Primekss, **concrete floors for factories**, Baiba Griezena and Janis Kamars.

878–881. Hewlett-Packard, makers of **printer** at steel factory, Cynthia "Cider" Lyons, Timothy Harms, Kejda Herzog, and Kara Sakuda.

882–884. Makers of **roofing for steel plants**, A.W. Kuettel and Sons, including Scott Privette, Jesse Smalley, and Ryan Mackey.

885–887. Harsco Metals and Minerals, which provides **additives for steelmaking**, including Joe Burkey, Bryan Turner, and Fred Schinke.

888–890. The folks at Pregis, which makes **bubble cushioning for shipping** coffee appliances, including Michael Jakubowski, Michael Briestansky, and Trent Elder.

891–893. CombineNet, **software for supply chains**, including Dean Arnold, Miles Krivoshia, and Jack Martin.

894–896. John Deere, which makes **tractor equipment** used at the steel plant, including Tom Swanson, Jenna Scheider, and Kaylee Vieira.

897–903. **Tree farmers**, including Albert and Wynette Shaw, Harry Hanna, Joe Hanna, Lee Youngblood, Nelson Vinson, and Terry Vinson.

904–908. Husqvarna, makers of **industrial chainsaws**, Darrell Engle, Jamie Krueger, Quantre Oglesby, Brian Bollinger, and Bobby Miller.

909–910. Makers of the **walkie-talkies** used in several factories and the reservoir along the chain, including Motorola's Soumee Datta Roy and Sara Abadi.

CHAPTER 8
THE FARMERS

911-918. **Farmers who grew the coffee beans**, Wilson, Wilmer, Yimi, Alexis, Jose, Javier, Neir, and Yabed Guarnizo.

919-922. Rainforest Alliance, which **gives the environmental certification** to the Guarnizo coffee, including Matthew Synder, Donita Dooley, Kiku Loomis, and Sabrina Vigilante.

923-924. Fritz Haber and Carl Bosch, **co-inventors of the nitrogen fixation process**, which makes modern farming possible.

925-926. Economists and others who helped **create Fairtrade certification**, Nico Roozen and Frans van der Hoff.

927-930. Cathie Aime, Steve Savage, John Vandermeer, and Jaime Castillo Zapata—academics **studying how to battle coffee rust** disease at various universities.

931-933. Carrie Silver, Eric Eldridge, Allison Schilling at MDA **weather systems**, used by farmers for predictions.

934. Hernando Duque at Fedecafé, which is the Colombia **federation of coffee farmers** that supports the growers.

935-938. Coffee Quality Institute, nonprofit **helping small coffee farms** in Colombia and elsewhere, including John Moore, Chris Hallien, Kimberly Easson, and Douglas Carpenter.

939. Father Francisco Romero, nineteenth-century **Colombian priest who prescribed planting coffee trees** to his flock as penance for confessed sins, helping start Colombian coffee industry.

940-942. Pinhalense, makers of the **coffee fruit de-pulping machine**, including Fabio Raimundo, Elizio Perini Cuzzuol, and Diego Ribeiro.

943-945. Plásticos Rimax, Colombian company that **makes bins** that store coffee in Colombia, including Daniel Martinez Ferro, Luis Barajas, and Lorena Salas.

946-948. Gehaka, **makers of PH meters** used in Colombia coffee plant, including Priscila Cursino Robayo, Fernando Engelbrecht, and Christian Kaufmann.

949-951. International Coffee Organization, intergovernmental **organization that brings together governments from importing and exporting nations**, including Christoph Sänger, Denis Seudieu, and Gerardo Patacconi.

952–955. The folks at Bühler Group, which makes the equipment used in Colombia to **sort coffee beans**, including Lisa Wasserman, Jaimie Larson, Brian Lieske, and Derek Miller.

I also need to thank the many folks who help me with my job so that I have money to pay for my cup of coffee every day.

956–965. Several people **read the manuscript** and provided excellent feedback, including Peter Griffin, Lynette Vanderwarker, Shannon Barr, Kristen Lasky, Beryl Jacobs, Willy Ramos, Douglas Stanley, Cole Kelly, Kevin Roose, and Candice Braun.

966–982. There are plenty to thank at Simon & Schuster, the **publisher of my books**, including this one, such as Jon Karp, Ben Loehnen, Amar Deol, Dana Trocker, Carolyn Reidy, Richard Rohrer, Marie Florio, Jeff Wilson, Alison Forner, Lisa Erwin, Michael Noble, Tiffany Frarey, Lauren Pires, Lisa Healy, Mara Lurie, Sybil Pincus, and Sherry Wasserman.

983–988. I want to give credit to the **mentors who gave me my big breaks**, including Rob Weisbach (my first editor), Steve Lipson (hired me at the *Antioch Daily Ledger*), Peter Kaplan, Maggie Murphy, Don Lemon, and David Granger.

989–1,013. The staff at TED, which **copublished this book and set up the related TED talk**, including my editor Michelle Quint, Alejandra Vasquez, Alex Hofmann, Mike Femia, Sacha Vega, Crawford Hunt, Cloe Shasha, Corey Hajim, Alex Moura, David Biello, Chee Pearlman, Helen Walters, Lorena Aviles, Tim Aumiller, Sioban Massiah, Sierra Paller, Briar Goldberg, Francisco Diez, Dana Viltz, Laurie House, Andrew Davis, and Stephen Robbins. And the people at MGMT Design, including Sarah Gephart, Ian Keliher, and Alicia Cheng.

1,014. And thank you to my **mother**. Every morning, my mom and I send each other an email listing something we're grateful for. Could be simply a comfortable pair of gloves. Could be the health of her grandkids. I find it enormously helpful. So in addition to giving birth to me, thank you, Mom, for doing this ritual with me.

1,015. Psychologist Scott Barry Kaufman wanted to make sure he credited Robert Emmons, who did a lot of **gratitude research** that helped with Kaufman's insights.

1,016–1,019. Also, some of the folks at LinkedIn who helped us **track down** people who had a role in my coffee, including Konstantin Guericke, Jean-Luc Vaillant, Allen Blue, and Eric Ly.

1,020–1,022. We kept track of my thankees on Google Sheets, so thanks to **developers** Sam Schillace, Steve Newman, and Claudia Carpenter.

1,023. Especially Riki Markowitz, who was a **tireless researcher** who helped me put together this list of thankees.

1,024–1,027. As well as **her family**, Mike Jimmy Markowitz, Marcel Markowitz, Ellie Carmella Markowitz, and Bruno, who kept her going when we were at 823 names and didn't think we could get a single one more.

1,028–1,031. The **reasons I get up in the morning to have my coffee**, my sons Jasper, Zane, and Lucas, and my wife, Julie.

ABOUT THE AUTHOR

A.J. Jacobs is the author of *The New York Times* bestsellers *Drop Dead Healthy*, *The Year of Living Biblically*, *My Life as an Experiment*, and *The Know-It-All*. Jacobs is a contributor to NPR, and has written for *The New York Times*, *The Washington Post*, and *Entertainment Weekly*. He lives in New York City with his wife, Julie, and their children. Visit him at AJJacobs.com and follow him on Twitter @ajjacobs.

WATCH A.J. JACOBS'S TED TALK

A.J. Jacobs's TED Talk, available for free at TED.com, is the companion to *Thanks a Thousand*.

PHOTO: RYAN LASH/TED

RELATED TALKS

A.J. Jacobs
The world's largest family reunion . . . we're all invited!
You may not know it yet, but A.J. Jacobs is probably your cousin (many, many times removed). Using genealogy websites, he's been following the unexpected links that make us all, however distantly, related. His goal: to throw the world's largest family reunion. See you there?

David Steindl-Rast
Want to be happy? Be grateful.
The one thing all humans have in common is that each of us wants to be happy, says Brother David Steindl-Rast, a monk and interfaith scholar. And happiness, he suggests, is born from gratitude. An inspiring lesson in slowing down, looking where you're going, and above all, being grateful.

Malcolm Gladwell
Choice, happiness, and spaghetti sauce
The Tipping Point author Malcolm Gladwell gets inside the food industry's pursuit of the perfect spaghetti sauce—and makes a larger argument about the nature of choice and happiness.

Candy Chang
Before I die I want to . . .
In her New Orleans neighborhood, artist and TED Fellow Candy Chang turned an abandoned house into a giant chalkboard asking a fill-in-the-blank question: "Before I die I want to _____." Her neighbors' answers—surprising, poignant, funny—became an unexpected mirror for the community. (What's your answer?)

Rescue
by David Miliband

We are in the midst of a global refugee crisis. Sixty-five million people are fleeing for their lives. The choices are urgent, not just for them but for all of us. What can we possibly do to help?

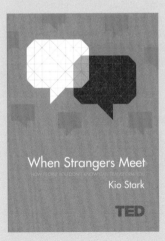

When Strangers Meet
by Kio Stark

Kio Stark invites you to discover the unexpected pleasures and exciting possibilities of talking to people you don't know. Stark reveals how these simple, surprising encounters push us toward greater openness and tolerance—and also how these fleeting but powerful emotional connections can change you, and the world we share.

In Praise of Wasting Time
by Alan Lightman

In today's frenzied and wired world, we are obsessed with the idea of not "wasting time." But have we lost the silences and solitude so essential to our inner lives?

The Misfit's Manifesto
by Lidia Yuknavitch

By reclaiming and celebrating the word misfit, this manifesto makes a powerful case for not fitting in—for recognizing the beauty, and difficulty, in forging an original path.

TED is a nonprofit devoted to spreading ideas, usually in the form of short, powerful talks (eighteen minutes or less) but also through books, animation, radio programs, and events. TED began in 1984 as a conference where Technology, Entertainment, and Design converged, and today covers almost every topic— from science to business to global issues—in more than 100 languages. Meanwhile, independently run TEDx events help share ideas in communities around the world.

TED is a global community, welcoming people from every discipline and culture who seek a deeper understanding of the world. We believe passionately in the power of ideas to change attitudes, lives, and, ultimately, our future. On TED.com, we're building a clearinghouse of free knowledge from the world's most inspired thinkers—and a community of curious souls to engage with ideas and each other, both online and at TED and TEDx events around the world, all year long.

In fact, everything we do—from the TED Radio Hour to the projects sparked by the TED Prize, from the global TEDx community to the TED-Ed lesson series— is driven by this goal: How can we best spread great ideas?

TED is owned by a nonprofit, nonpartisan foundation.